20 APR 1999

Left-handed Man
in a
Right-handed World

Left-handed Man
in a
Right-handed World

By MICHAEL BARSLEY
with Illustrations by the Author

 Pitman Publishing

First published 1970

Sir Isaac Pitman and Sons Ltd
Pitman House, Parker Street, Kingsway, London, WC2B 5PB
P.O. Box 6038, Portal Street, Nairobi, Kenya
Sir Isaac Pitman (Pty) Aust. Ltd
Pitman House, Bouverie Street, Carlton, Victoria 3053, Australia
Pitman Publishing Company S.A. Ltd
P.O. Box 9898, Johannesburg, S. Africa
Pitman Publishing Corporation
6 East 43rd Street, New York, N.Y. 10017, U.S.A.
Sir Isaac Pitman (Canada) Ltd
Pitman House, 381–383 Church Street, Toronto, 3, Canada
The Copp Clark Publishing Company
517 Wellington Street, Toronto, 2B, Canada

ISBN: 0 273 40139 4

Printed in Great Britain
by Ebenezer Baylis & Son Limited
The Trinity Press, Worcester, and London
G0 – (G.3791)

To Jenny, the Helping Hand

Preface

Left-handers and right-handers alike have encouraged me, a left-hander, in this further survey of sinistrals—an unhappy name for the 8 to 10 per cent of the world population who have to exist in a world largely run for right-handers. My particular thanks are due to those who have sent many suggestions and personal case-histories which prove the point of this book, and the value of having a Left-Handers' Association in Britain where these points can be raised. (There is, I am glad to note, a similar organization in the United States.)

The British sinistral association has, among several practical aims, such as a belief that left-handed writing should be allowed in schools in *all* countries (in the majority it is forbidden, or at least discouraged, even to this day), a recommendation to remove "the slur of the centuries against the left-hander in language, lore, superstition and religion." To quote one small instance: recently a book appeared in the U.S., reprinted for Britain, entitled *The Left-Handed Dictionary*. It proved to have nothing to do with left-handedness at all, but was a collection of "hip definitions that once tripped gaily off forked tongues." Then followed a host of contributors. In other words, a collection of "left-handed" compliments. This is the sort of derogatory treatment we sinistrals can do without. Once the right-hander *recognizes* the existence of the left-hander, he sees him everywhere. The first shot in the sinistro-dextral war has been fired, and, who knows, Left Power may be on the way.

In preparing this survey, I have been in touch with many authorities and local bodies as well as with individuals, and it would be impossible to identify them all, but I acknowledge the help and advice given by Dr. Macdonald Critchley, of the National Hospital for Nervous Diseases, London; Professor Oliver Zangwill of the Cambridge University Psychological Laboratory; Dr. J. Drewson of the Institute of Experimental Psychology, Oxford; M. le

7

Professeur H. Desoille, President of the Société de Médecine de Travail de France; Mrs. S. Naidoo, of the Word Blindness Centre, Coram Fields, London; Mr. Moller of Parker Pen Co. Ltd.; Mr. Frank Shaw of the Scouse Press, Liverpool; Mr. Michael Flanders, who freely gave permission to reprint the words of his sinistral song *Misalliance*.

I am especially indebted to Mr. and Mrs. William Gruby, both right-handers, who have taken up the cause of the sinistral with their Left-Handed Shop, and to Mr. James T. de Kay, of New York, author and illustrator of his own Left-Handed Book, who wrote in my copy: "No army is strong enough to withstand a great idea when its time has come."

The left-handed illustrations are, with the exception of those copied in museums, my own. In some cases they may seem to have little relevance to the text, but at least they represent the feelings of left-handed man in this right-handed world.

Inevitably some statistics and material have been quoted from my previous *Left-Handed Book*, and I wish to thank Mr. Ernest Hecht and the Souvenir Press. Thanks are also due to the following publishers for permission to use copyright material in quotation: Penguin Books Ltd. (*The Ambidextrous Universe*, by Martin Gardner); University of London Press, Ltd. (Sir Cyril Burt and Dr. Margaret Clark); Macmillan & Co. (Sir John Wheeler-Bennett); Chapman and Hall Ltd. (C. S. Orton); Pitman Medical Publishing Co. (Dr. Macdonald Critchley); Lothrop, Lee Shepard Co., Boston (Dr. Ira S. Wile); to Robert Graves (*The Greek Myths*); and to the Executors of the Estate of the late H. G. Wells (*Mr. Britling Sees it Through*).

MICHAEL BARSLEY

London—Oxford

Contents

The Case for the Left-hander

There are many minority groups among mankind and have been since the followers of Baal who built the Golden Calf, the Children of Israel who went into captivity in Egypt, the Early Christians who defied the power of Rome, the *Mayflower* pilgrims who left Plymouth for the New World, the Jehovah's Witnesses defying orthodox Christianity, the Rechabites, the Mormons, the Vegetarians, the Bahais, the Flat-Earth Society, the Hippies—deciding to go their own way and take their chance on their beliefs and way of life.

But these are minorities which deliberately adopt a way of life. No fundamentalist, no spiritualist, is bound by nature to exist as such. By contrast, no spastic, no person born blind, deaf or dumb, or mentally handicapped, no thalidomide or mongol child asks for their state to be such as it is. The seeds are there, for mankind to reveal, to regret, and to redress where possible.

There is one minority, however, which experts consider may amount to one-tenth of the world population and which has until recently been ignored—indeed, despised down the centuries—the man or woman born with a natural preference for the left hand, the left foot, and other adjacencies.

It was W. S. Gilbert who wrote (before the advent of the British Labour Party) in *Iolanthe*—

> For every boy and every girl
> That's born into this world alive,
> Is either a little Liberal,
> Or else a little Conservative.

It could be more practically argued that every boy and every girl, in every country (and this applies as much in Malaya, Malawi or Manchester) is born potentially either a little right-hander or a little left-hander.

Opening shot in the dextro–sinistral war

The various reasons are stated later in this book, which seeks once again to call attention to the left-hander, and his particular needs, many of which are largely neglected in a world which is predominantly right-handed in thought, word and deed.

No one would pretend that, in western society, the left-hander is any longer persecuted, as in the past. But while the needs of this perpetually recurring minority remain unconsidered, as is the case in many countries where children are forced to write right-handed in schools, and adopt other majority-rule practices, the fundamental wishes of the sinistral should not only be respected, but encouraged, to allow full development.

In one human field—that of sport—there have been no restrictions, from the days of the left-handed gladiator in the Roman arena to the supremacy of left-handed cricketers, baseball players, lawn-tennis champions, and fencers.

Why, if the sporting impulse of the sinistral be permitted, should not other characteristics be encouraged, particularly in education, and in the use of household goods and machinery?

This is a right-handed world, sanctioned not only by a right-handed majority but by the very use of the language itself, as formed by a species related to ambidextral monkeys, gorillas and chimpanzees. In most human languages, the word for a left-hander or left-handedness has a derogatory meaning, implying weakness or evil. There are few left-handed heroes. All gods are right-handed, and in the Christian New Testament it is sad to see that the notorious anti-left speaker is that otherwise tolerant Son of God, Jesus Christ Himself. Left-handed Christians could not be expected to forgive Jesus, if it were not that the words of St. Matthew the taxgatherer were obviously used many years later, particularly to justify the Muslim belief in the Clean and Unclean Hand, and the association of the Devil with Sinistrality.

I have often tried to point out the appalling consequences of this unfortunate Parable of the Sheep and the Goats at the Day of Judgement (Matthew, Chapter xxv) but without apparently convincing the complacent right-handed majority that the sinistrals have a case to answer which has been in operation for centuries, and has always been in their disfavour.

To Hell, I would say, with right-handers who do not recognize

*Plutarch and Adler both noted
that left-handers tend to cross
the left leg over the right*

the left-handed minority. To Hell, because Hell was where sinistral Satan dwelt, with the goats, while the sheep lived in Heaven with the Good Shepherd. There have been many different versions of the Bible, from the "Breeches" Bible to the latest modernized University Edition. If Christian left-handers are to feel that they are fully members of Christ's church (He sat on the right hand of God, and all the left-hander has is the Holy Ghost) this prejudice in favour of one hand against another must be got rid of.

Is there something distinctive or peculiar about left-handers which is outwardly noticeable? In some of their actions, obviously so. If you are sitting in a railway carriage, writing left-handedly, you are still likely to get a puzzled stare from one or two of your fellow-passengers, even in Britain. In Germany the stares would be still more puzzled, for the *linkser* is a rarity there. Move further, out of Europe into the Middle East, and you will often find mild astonishment as you fill in papers at an airport in say, Morocco or Syria. "At first," one Middle-Eastern official remarked, "one thinks they must have suffered some sort of injury."

There are other outward signs, not so important or significant: a telephone at the right ear; a cup or trophy presented with the left hand; a cigarette or glass held in the left hand in a restaurant; applauding hands, in which the left hand smites the right. Left-handed people instinctively cross their left leg over the right, and right-handed people do the opposite. (In these days of the mini-skirt, an investigator can enjoy the observation, whichever way it goes!)

The inward characteristics of the left-hander are less easy to determine. He represents, as we know, an eight to ten per cent minority in the world as a whole. Treatment of him varies from country to country, from tribe to tribe. But what is he like, from the expert's point of view?

"Left-handed people," declared Lawson G. Lowrey, of the American Orthopsychiatric Association, "have often been described as temperamental, unstable, unintelligent, stubborn, pugnacious, and so on through a list of undesirable personality attributes. What those who thus castigate left-handed people have overlooked, is that all these personality traits also occur in right-handed people and, when quantitative measurements are possible, in approximately the same proportions in both groups."

For this relief much thanks. Sir Cyril Burt offers this further explanation, in his book, *The Backward Child*.

"Although I have no conclusive figures to offer, all my experience confirms the impression that, when temperament and left-handedness are intimately related, the peculiarities and neurotic symptoms generally take what I have called the sthenic, aggressive form rather than the asthenic or submissive. Again and again in my own case-summaries, the left-handed child has been described as stubborn and wilful. At times he is visibly of an assertive type, domineering, over-bearing, and openly rebellious against the dictates of authority. But more often his aggressive tendencies are concealed or repressed: and the child belongs to a class well known to practising psychiatrists and familiarly dubbed by them 'obstinate introverts.' Analysis or psycho-analysis will sometimes show that the left-handedness itself rests on an unconscious neurotic compulsion: the dogged adherence to a perverse way of writing symbolizes, as it were, a secret desire to defy all conventions. . . . Even left-handed girls, as a little watchfulness will show, often possess a strong, self-willed, almost masculine disposition: by many little tell-tale symptoms, besides the clumsy management of their hands—by their careless dress, their ungainly walk, their tomboy tricks and mannerisms—they mutely display a private scorn for the canons of feminine grace and elegance."

Burt was writing in 1937, when most girls were just girls, heaven be praised, and grew up into lush womanhood. Today, oddly enough, some of them seem to exhibit just what he has been describing. Many of today's teenage "birds," with their exhibitionism, their assertiveness, their awareness of being wanted, not so much by parents or boy-friends as by press, TV, and boutique-owners, show to the world their bruised and blazing eyes and flaunt their physical attractions—and their earning power. Every chick has a chequebook. But this is a characteristic of both left-handed and right-handed young women, and is largely a matter of social and financial change in the world, when the emphasis is on being young and brazen and solvent. There has not yet, to my knowledge, been a survey of the proportion of left-handers among the hippies and pot-takers and pill-swallowers in our present generation, to find out if the sinistrals are among the leaders.

"Among children of school age," Burt concludes, "three main factors seem to stand out—heredity, habit, and a half unconscious perversity. The old-fashioned teacher was not wholly unjustified in assuming that, when his left-hand pupils declined to use their right hands, it wasn't because they couldn't, but because they wouldn't."

Dr. Abram Blau, another distinguished authority, chief psychiatrist at New York University Clinic, summed up the characteristics of the left-hander in terms which should make any sinistral's blood boil, and lead to an immediate bid for Left Power. His book *The Master Hand*, published in 1946, is an interesting and learned work, devoted largely to advice for parents about their left-handed children. But he has this to say about sinistrality in general.

"The origin can be explained as a deviation in the learning process which normally leads to dextrality, and can be divided into three types: due to an inherent deficiency, physical or mental; due to faulty education; due to emotional negativism."

"H'm, Dr. Blau says that sinistrality is nothing more than an expression of infantile negativism, springing from a contrary emotional attitude to the learning of right-handedness"

No mention of the fact that, when left alone, a child *naturally* favours one hand or the other. However, the sting is in the characteristics which Dr. Blau ascribes to the luckless minority. "Personality," he begins, "is the sum total of what the person is, and presents to the world as a result of his physical and mental functioning."

Agreed. At a later stage, in dealing with the young child's dependence on parental influence, he adds "character is *made*; it does not just happen!" words which have fallen so often from the lips of headmasters and headmistresses in public schools of high rank and strict discipline.

We must be fair to Dr. Blau who, as explained elsewhere, believes that children who have the temerity to show signs of sinistrality should be switched, but not forcibly. But his insistence on the negative qualities of the average left-hander, leaving aside both the genius and the mental defective, brings him to this conclusion—

"The sinistral himself must become cognizant in early life that he is abnormal and a sort of misfit in this right-handed world." He goes on to cite the many handicaps which form part of this book. He is very sympathetic. Like the Walrus, he weeps for us. But then—just look at our characteristics—

"Some of the outstanding features of the character type are obstinacy, inordinate orderliness, parsimony, rigidity, a tendency to over-intellectualization, and self-wilfulness."

How now, Abram Blau! How many benefits and adornments to society have been given to a right-handed world which gave us such

"You've a right to be left!"

staunch dextrals as Hitler, Mussolini, and Stalin? Left-handers may be negative, and recessive, and not aspire to power (the last left-handed dictator is said to have been Julius Caesar, and before him, on rather vague authority, Alexander the Great). We do not wish to sweep the world (if indeed the world is worth sweeping). We leave that to the right-handers—and one may grieve over what they've done so far. Only in the world of sport has the left hand "gotten the victory." "Man, if not nature," wrote Dr. Ira S. Wile, "has built up a world of righteous right-handedness."

Sun-worship
and Religion

A definition of sun-worship—The sun-gods described—Assyria, Egypt, North-American Indians, Incas, Buddhists, Christians—Greek mythology and Uranus—Augury, Greek and Roman—The left side becomes the unlucky one—Christianity and handedness—Prejudice in the Bible— The Tribe of Benjamin—The scapegoat—Parable of the right-handed Sheep and the left-handed Goats—Christian practice today

From the dawn of time—and "dawn" is literally the appropriate word—man worshipped the sun, as the source of light and warmth. Primitive man rose in the morning, and though he had no outward act of worship, his instinct would be to turn and look towards the bright golden orb in the sky. As Dr. Wile puts it: "with the daily advent of that orb, man felt more safe, and he was grateful. Thus began a new homage, and man faced the east, his anxious eyes following through its course via the south to its glorious extinction in the west. If there was a sun cure in those days, man would have been right by turning himself to the right, ever in the course of the sun. This, of course, applies to those who lived in the northern hemisphere, but they have always been greatly in the majority."

From observation came adoration. Whole tribes were affected by the position of the sun. Migrations took place to discover the ideal place to live in relation to the sun's rays. It is not a far cry from these early days to the trial of Galileo, who murmured "Eppur si muove" (and yet it does move) when forced to deny that the earth moved round the sun. Then came the vision of the sun-god. When pyramids and temples were built, by the Egyptians, they faced the rising sun. Apollo was a sun-god: so, in their own interpreted way, were Horus, Indra, and Krishna. The Japanese worshipped the sun as a living God. Pilgrims would ascend the sacred Mount Fuji, to offer prayers as the first rays of the sun could be seen.

The Assyrians are said to have introduced sun-worship in the Middle East.

> *The Assyrians came down like a wolf on the fold,*
> *And their cohorts were gleaming with purple and gold.* . . .

These proud people, though they eventually came to destruction, influenced the Persians and Phoenicians with their sun-god Baal. The Phoenicians "stretched their hands towards the sun; for him they thought the only Lord of Heaven; calling him Beelsamin, which in Phoenician is Lord of Heaven, but in Greek, Zeus." In Persia, Zoroaster was the prophet. He decreed that there were two opposing gods, one of light (Ormazd) the other of darkness (Ahriman). As mediator between the two he appointed Mithras. The subsequent history of Mithras has become popular knowledge. He was the god of the Roman soldier, and the discovery of a temple dedicated to him, underground in the City of London in 1954, gave evidence of this type of worship.

Zeus the sun-god has a parallel with Jehovah the god of Israel. Later we shall see how Christianity, in its ritual practices, followed the movements of the sun worshipper, until Jesus said, "I am the Light of the World," summing up in those few words the aspirations of those who worshipped the Sun, first as an object, then as a personalized Being.

In Egypt the god was Ra, the sun. From this short title came Pharaoh, the "Son of the Sun God." When the children of Israel were in captivity there for eighteen years, we do not know what kind of worship they practised, in private or in secret, but they must have seen all the intricacies of the Egyptian cults, most of which concerned the sun, as sacred, and evil as darkness, and the Jewish imagery is largely derived from such a source. After the return to Palestine, it was Moses who fought against and prohibited sun-worship by such peoples as the tribe of Manasseh, the Philistines— who also had two goddesses of Evil and Lust, Ashtaroth and Astarte —with their god Dagon, and the worshippers of Baal.

On the other side of the world, the North-American Indians also indulged in sun-worship ceremonies, which involved hand usage

Marduk, Babylonian God with
Tramet, Demon of the Waters

Mexican God

Egypt: Horus the Younger
with Flail and Dove of the
Holy Spirit

Mexico

Atum the Creator, Mexico

Egyptian God Amsu

Anubis, Dog God of Egypt

Shiva, India: "I've only got three pairs of hands!"

and preference. Chieftains of Red Indian tribes usually took a title which had some connection with being a relation of the sun, or even the sun himself.

The Dakotahs, who originated in Mexico, where an elaborate form of sun-worship existed, have left behind a whole history of ritual and dances, such as the Sun Dance, which was only discontinued in 1883. It was in honour of the sun-god Wakantanka.

Similarly, the Incas staged their elaborate ceremonies facing the east and made their sacrifices at the propitious hour of dawn (as in Stonehenge in England). Their temples were constructed to face the east. This practice was repeated with nearly all the early peoples of the world—the Ainus who preceded the Japanese, the Caucasians, the Mayas, the Muslims whose Mecca was eastward, the Greeks—the list is endless. There are two interesting exceptions. One, the Chinese, the oldest civilization on earth, who did not apparently regard the sun as a god (the "Thoughts" of Mao-Tse-Tung do not give King Sol any credit at all—but then, he is against worship as well as royalty).

The Buddhist conception of the universe was based on the two cosmic principles called Ying and Yan. Ying guarded the south, with a Red Bird as its symbol, and was regarded as the positive male element. Yan, symbolized by a tortoise, was guardian of the north, and was the negative female element. Thus aerial and earth, in the electrical sense, were the source of life, and together made the ultimate in a circle called the Tao, a symbol more venerated by the Chinese than today's Mao (if that is possible). The Buddha made clear that there were two roads through life: the left road, which is fraught with peril and is of ill omen; and the eightfold right path, which is of good omen. Much importance was attached to the prayer wheel, which always rotated to the right. To many, the opposing forces of Ying and Yan seem to make more sense than sun-worship, and it is perhaps significant that the three discoverers of an element of non-symmetry in the Universe were all of Chinese origin.

The other partial exception to the all-out worship of the sun god lies in India. True, Krishna was regarded as a sun-god, but it was the divided caste system—into the left and right caste—which dominated much of the Hindu religion.

Christianity received its sun-worship and sun-symbols from

several different religions. It was to contribute original ideas later, but the constant references to the sun are significant. The Early Christians called their baptism the "Illumination." Christ was the Sun of Righteousness and so on. All this involved the idea that the East, home of the rising sun, was the sacred area.

Left-handers, in defending themselves against charges of being peculiar, cussed, non-conforming, weak, or just plain evil, should arm themselves with some knowledge of the sun and the part it has played in the emergence of religion and religious habits. As for the Moon, it has become merely the plaything of the Earth.

Uranus, a Figure of Greek myth, represented Heaven, one of the figures emerging from Earth (Gaea). The union of Heaven and Earth was disturbed when they had seven offspring—of whom the youngest was called Cronus. They were the Titans. From Robert Graves, in *Greek Myths*, we learn what happened to Uranus—

"Uranus fathered the Titans upon Mother Earth, after he had thrown his rebellious sons, the Cyclops, into Tartarus, a gloomy place in the Underworld . . . In revenge, Mother Earth persuaded the Titans to attack their father, and they did so, led by Cronus, the youngest of the seven whom she armed with a flint sickle. They surprised Uranus as he slept, and it was with the flint sickle that the merciless Cronus castrated him, grasping his genitals with the left hand (which has ever since been the hand of ill-omen) and afterwards throwing them, and the sickle too, into the sea by Cape Drepanum."

The *Encyclopaedia Britannica* takes up the story, describing how the drops of blood formed the Erinyes, the Giants, and the Nymphs. From the severed member as it floated in the sea sprang, surprisingly, Aphrodite—"Dame Venus, love's lady, was born of the sea"—but what an origin!

The legend is said to be of barbaric, pre-Greek origin, perhaps Oriental or Hittite. Cronus had separated Heaven and Earth by his action, and only until he had been similarly treated by Zeus was the marriage of Heaven and Earth, a subject of so much poetry, restored.

Augury means prophecy, either good or bad. But originally the word came from a type of man who today would be among that popular and well-paid group, the horoscope readers and predictors, figuring prominently in newspapers and magazines, giving Pisces and Virgo and the others advice on whether to make a journey or

have a romantic affair or try a financial deal. Very few people take
such predictions very seriously today, and very few of the modern
augurs have much ground on which to base their prophecies. A good
augur will tell you that conditions for one Zodiacal person can only
be predicted by linking his sign of the Zodiac by its relation with
another sign. Some augurs predict the time of major events, such as
war or change of government or national disaster, though it seems
that all of them missed out on the timing of the late Major Gagarin's
first leap into outer space. But it is still a profitable line of business.

The Roman augurs, however, were a religious college, not commercial individuals, and they play an important part in the distinction
between right and left, and the merits thereof. The left-hander should
certainly be acquainted with a few facts, for use when in discussion
with right-handers, who are apt to use words like "sinister" under
the bland assumption that it always meant evil. This is not so. The
Roman word for left hand was *laeva*—"sinister" was merely the
left side of a shield.

Consider, then, the Roman augur in his magnificent toga with
bright scarlet stripes, bordered in purple, holding his *lituus*, a staff
free from knots and bent at the top. Before consulting the will of
Jupiter, he would have to mark out a consecrated space, just as
wizards described their circle "widdershins," and put up a tent.
The important thing to remember is that the Roman augurs in the
early days faced south, and the east (i.e. left side) was then considered more propitious and favourable than the west or right side.
The augurs of Greece, an older civilization, faced north, and
consequently the left was the unlucky side. This was confirmed by
Plato, Plutarch and Aristotle. Yet the Romans conquered the Greeks.
Why, then, did not the left continue to be good, and the right, bad?
It might have altered the whole history of handedness. Think of it!
Left-handers would continue to be a minority, biologically, in the
same ratio as today, but they might have been, by their auspicious
Roman origins, an exclusive and exalted minority.

But the sinistral élite never came about, since the Greek position,
facing the magnetic north, became adopted by the Roman augurs,
and the left lost its pre-eminent position.

There were five signs which the gods might give. The first,
lightning (if left to right, favourable). At this, the whole Assembly

(Parliament) rose for the day—lucky for them. There was complete faith in the augurs' report, and at times these exalted men were said to have pretended to spot that the flash came from that particular direction, in order to have the session suspended at the plea of one faction of senator friends. It is quite probable that Cicero, once an augur himself, and a senator, must often have been tempted to resort to this stratagem. The second divination was the flight of birds, again the left-to-right movement being the favourable one. It was on this form of prophecy that Rome was named. Romulus stood on one hill, Remus on another, and one solitary bird, flying in from the east, gave him authority to found the city, which might otherwise have been called after Remus.

The remaining prophecies do not concern left and right: they were the droppings of birds, various signs made by animals, and various miscellaneous forebodings, such as the ill-luck of meeting a raven when you left your house (the raven, like the goat, never had any luck).

Sad it is, therefore, that the augurs turned from south to north. The results were tremendous. The word sinister became evil. The left-handed minority didn't even have luck on its side. The Christian and other religions based all their ritual on right-handedness and turning to meet the sun. The devil became a left-footed goat.

If there is any body of men who should be despised by left-handers, it is the turncoat Roman augurs.

It is very necessary for every left-hander to acquaint himself with the attitude of orthodox Christianity towards the left hand and left-handers, for if the letter of the Old and New Testaments be observed, there is not much hope, morally, for sinistrals. And since, at the latest estimate, there are about 900 million followers of Jesus Christ on earth (that is an official figure: how far most of them follow and how fervently is a matter for speculation—perhaps no more than 10 per cent) the preaching and the practice are important.

Derived partly from sun-worship and circumambulation and adopted by the Romans, Christianity is on a par with most other religions in favouring the right hand in thought, word, and deed.

Most religions—with the exception of such faiths as the Quakers, the Druses and the Bahais—rely on a ritual as well as a faith. The faith is easy to fathom. There are over one hundred favourable

references to the right hand in the Bible, and about twenty-five
unfavourable references to the left. The only left-hander chosen by
Jehovah to deliver the children of Israel from bondage was Ehud,
of the tribe of Benjamin, who took the fat king Eglon of Moab by
surprise by stabbing him, at a private audience, with a dagger
strapped on his right thigh (the Moabite guards had obviously only
searched him for weapons on the *left* side). The Benjamites were also
famous for their commando force of 700 left-handed slingers. "Every
one," it says in the Book of Judges, "could sling stones at an hair's
breadth, and not miss." A sore trouble indeed they were to the
Israelites, and the Lord allowed them to inflict great casualties on his
Chosen People, until He decided that enough was enough, and had
the tribe of Benjamin well-nigh wiped out, slingers and all. They
were, however, replenished by a plentiful supply of Israelite virgins,
and the tribe lived on to include Saul, David, and Jonathan among
its members. It is an astonishing chapter in Old Testament history:
one that the left-hander must never forget. But the Psalms of David
give little comfort to the sinistral.

"If I forget thee, O Jerusalem, let my right hand forget its
cunning . . . "; "I have set the Lord always before me: because he is
at my right hand, I shall not be moved . . . "; "The Lord's right
hand, and his holy arm, hath gotten him the victory . . . "; "The
Lord said unto my lord, sit thou at my right hand, until I make
thine enemies thy footstool . . . ."

The quotations proliferate: their name is legion. Their origin
is a mixture of Egyptian, Phoenician and Arabian superstition,
coupled with the undoubted fact that God was invariably on the
side of the big battalions—the right-handers, who were presumably
being born in the same ratio to left-handers as today, if one accepts
that handedness is hereditary. Among animals singled out as evil,
the chief culprit was the goat, condemned by Aaron, in the book of
Leviticus, to be a sin offering (a scapegoat, in fact) to "bear the sins
of the world." Anyone who has seen Holman Hunt's picture, "The
Scapegoat," will know how miserable the animal can look.

At this stage of the inquiry, the left-hander must beware, because
all too soon will come the evidence of the New Testament, and the
words allegedly spoken by Jesus, whom none of the 900 million
Christians in the world are supposed to question or contradict.

Parable of sheep and goats

Christianity is a religion founded in the Middle East. Initially, it had nothing to do with Europe, with the Vatican, Bach's *St. Matthew Passion*, or with the paintings of Italy, France, and Germany, or the icons of the independent churches of Greece and Russia.

Let us consider the Goat first. It was allowed to go "as a scapegoat into the wilderness." It was obviously an unpopular animal because it ate everything in sight; unlike the sheep, the Christian's favourite animal, which safely grazed and produced wool. The shepherd was the hero: the goatherd was never mentioned. It was the shepherds that watched their flocks by night, all seated on the ground. It was the Parable of the Lost Sheep which proved to be one of the most popular of the Parables of Jesus. "Feed my sheep," He said. The Lamb of God, the Paschal Lamb, took away the sins of the world, just as, presumably, the wicked goat received them, as punishment.

Any impartial student of this situation must consider two things. The goat was shunned because it was regarded as a voracious and vicious animal—rather like the fox is regarded today. It was linked, as a hoofed animal, with the god Pan. And whatever the great god Pan was doing, down in the reeds by the river, he was obviously up to no good: he was "spreading ruin and scattering ban."

The second consideration is that every religion must have its devil as well as its god. The more Christianity advances in wisdom and recognition of its past faults and misinterpretations, the less important does the Devil become. To Milton, Satan was a fallen angel, but in man's shape, and he emerged almost as the hero-villain of *Paradise Lost*, urging his satanic followers to resist "the red right hand of God."

The main condemnation of the left lies in the Gospel according to St. Matthew. Here, in Chapter xxv, is written the Parable of the Sheep and the Goats, an account so entirely alien to the Jesus of the Sermon on the Mount in Galilee that, whatever scholars may say, it can be discounted as a damaging and dangerous example of mis-reporting. From it resulted, eventually, the separation, not only of the sheep and the goats but of the right from the left. Left-handers, once again, would do well to acquaint themselves with this parable, and interpret it by the spirit in which it was reported, by a middle-eastern disciple called Matthew, who, it would appear, "ghosted" the name of Jesus to suit the mood and superstition of the time.

The Vision of Judgement begins: "When the Son of Man shall come in his glory . . . he shall sit upon the throne of his glory . . . and before him shall be gathered all nations, and he shall separate them one from another, as a shepherd divideth his sheep from the goats. And he shall set the sheep on his right hand, and the goats on his left. . . . "

(Why, at this stage, should the goat be associated with the left? Ask your nearest curate, vicar, or bishop.)

"Then shall the King say unto them on his right hand, Come ye blessed of my Fathers, inherit the Kingdom prepared for you from the foundation of the world. . . .

"Then shall he say unto them on the left hand, Depart from me, ye cursed, into everlasting fire, prepared for the devil and his angels. . . . "

Could there be any more direct incitement against left-handers than this? It is as vindictive as one of Hitler's speeches against the Jews. It has been of immense value to all those who have connected the left-handed with the Satanic. It is Holy Writ: and it is wholly rubbish, and need not seriously be considered today. But it has done untold harm, in the past.

Jesus, who loved His enemies and forgave those who crucified Him, was not that sort of person. When He drove the money-changers from the Temple, that was another matter. When He failed to make a take-over bid for the young man "who had great possessions," that was again another matter. But the Vision of Judgement, and all the mumbo-jumbo about sheep and goats, is just a Middle-Eastern fable, and it should therefore be rejected by modern Christians, and the chapter be amended in the Bible, and not read in its original form in churches. It could give a left-hander (who is born left-handed, presumably by the will of God if not by any other means) a tremendous sense of inferiority, connected with the Devil and the goat. Why? Various explanations occur in my Devil's Dictionary, among them the superstition of the Unclean Hand, which may account for some of the gloss which has been added to the alleged words of Jesus. It is doubtful if He ever spoke the words of the Vision of Judgement. But the built-in image remained, and became a matter, not only of controversy but at times of life and death.

Christianity, originally a Middle-Eastern religion, represents neither West nor East, neither white nor coloured. If there is a super-God who, in considering this tiny planet-among-a-million planets, decided to start a practical but perfectionist life, personalized by His son Jesus, on this particular planet we call Earth, He might indeed have taken a pin and, blindfold, stuck it in the middle of our world. The place might well have turned out to be the city of Jerusalem, home of three of the great faiths of this world: Jewish, Muslim and Christian.

All these religious references seem to have nothing to do with handedness, but in fact they are very closely associated with it. Most religions must have a ritual, as we have said, just as the military have to have a routine, and surgery and hospitals have to keep to their own method of working. Therefore, the left-hander, out-numbered ten to one, must allow the right-hander to get on with his dextral religious roundabout. The sign of the cross is performed with the right hand, and the last two motions are left shoulder to right. The blessing is given with the right hand (though I know of one English bishop who, on being installed, gave it with his left hand, because as he said, "I had that damned stick [crozier] in my right hand"—and nobody noticed). At the communion service the elements have to be received as follows: the wafer to be accepted with the right palm, placed over the left palm: the chalice to be taken with the right hand, supported by the left as a subsidiary.

Well, for heaven's sake. One does not wish for anarchy to take place within the western churches as well as in the universities—better some ritual than none at all: better, perhaps, belief in the right-handedness of God than a perpetual struggle between the Left God and the Right—but, at least, the modern left-hander ought to be aware of the conditions under which, with the best will in the world, he or she can qualify to be a Christian, while utterly rejecting the unfortunate and damaging parable of the Sheep and the Goats.

"Pleased to meet you"
The Devil greets with the left hand

Manual and Speech Problems

Handwriting with its prejudice against left-handed writers—Pen-strokes, difficulty in performing—Reversed letters—Handwriting in other countries —Arabic and Jewish styles—Origins of handwriting—Mirror-writing— Left-handed drawing—Speech defects—Stammering and stuttering compared—Report by the University of Iowa—Professor Wendell Johnson's theory.

*H*andwriting, for the left-hander, is the heart of the matter. It is the main activity which distinguishes the sinistral part of humanity from the dextral. It has been in the past a serious cause of dissension among educational authorities. The dextro-sinistral war so often begins at school, where the natural, would-be left-hander is the odd boy out, or the odd girl out, a conspicuous and peculiar figure to both class and teacher alike.

One would suspect that much of the traditional prejudice against the would-be left-handed schoolboy was not so much against sinistrality as such—in line with the superstitions about the Devil and so on—as against a deviation from or a rebellion against conformity. Just as the military code has to be obeyed by one and all, exactly according to King's Regulations, so the attitude of school-teachers, harassed and underpaid though they may often be, has been to see that, in the earlier years, everyone toes the line and obeys the educational code. One of the items in that code has for centuries been that all pupils write with the right hand, and with their slates or exercise books upright. That at least was a step towards the peace which comes from conformity, and it was not observed that a left-handed writer needs to have his paper at a slant, since he is writing towards the body.

33

Left-handed writing positions

There are countless examples of punishments meted out, until recent years, to those who persisted in writing left-handedly. The odd boy out would be held up as an example to the form, and would no doubt acquire one of the numerous terms for a left-hander, according to the area in which he lived. Gradually this form of persecution ceased, in Western Europe and in the U.S. and Canada. A left-hander might become top of the class, and no one would say this was a victory for the Devil, or non-conformity. Ink-wells, always at the top right-hand corner of the desk (making it much harder for the left-hander, reaching out to dip his pen, not to blot his copy-book) disappeared, though the American school desk, with the arm-rest only on the right, continued until recent years, when a proportion of left arm-rests was introduced. Left-handed fountain pens, the ball-point and the felt-tip nib emancipated the left-hand writer from the problem of writing in a manner which could frequently tear the paper.

Cyril Burt has made some careful observations about pen-strokes. He, with other experts, agrees that the English language, as far as handwriting is concerned, is primarily intended for the right-hander. "The reasons are clear: first of all, it is easier to pull the pen than to push it; and secondly, the hand in moving thus does not obstruct the view of what is just written." Many left-handers adopt the style known as the "hook," in which the pen is held upright, but pointing downwards, so that what has been written is not covered. It is almost as fascinating to watch expert "hook" writing as to watch mirror writing, but the advantage of the former is that it is entirely readable.

"The easiest pen-stroke of all," Burt continues, "is a rapid line drawn obliquely outwards and upwards. With the right hand, this means moving away from the bottom left-hand corner and upwards to the top right-hand corner . . . most letters, in ordinary joined handwriting, begin with such a stroke. With the left hand, such a stroke is the most difficult of all; hence, if he is not exercising careful attention and control, the left-hander tends naturally to substitute a movement upwards towards the left and so begins his letters with a reversed or backward movement."

Left-handed children tend to reverse letters as a result. The most common are letters like *m*, *n*, *u*, and *e*. This sometimes extends to right-handed children as well. The letter *o* is the decisive case. A left-hander will instinctively describe a circle "widdershins" or anti-clockwise.

Abram Blau points out that in the eye-hand co-ordination of writing, only one eye is used. "Hand-writing involves the focus and alignment of three parts at the close range of reading: eye, hand (with pen) and paper. Such alignment is impossible with binocular vision because of the spacing of the two eyes. When an attempt is made to focus them simultaneously, the result is a double image of either the second or third part."

This is another argument for the definite requirement of a dominant eye.

But, if emancipation for left-handed children has come to the north-western hemisphere and Western Europe, the majority of countries still insist on right-handed conformity. One of the only things West and East Germany had in common until recently (apart from the Berlin Wall) was compulsory right-handed writing in schools. The West Germans now permit left-handed writing—but right-handed conformity, as far as the latest information can be obtained, is the rule in Spain, Italy, Yugoslavia, and in all the Iron Curtain countries, with the honourable exception of Czechoslovakia. Many of the Soviet Union's top athletes are left-handed (some are Olympic gold-medallists) but the right hand is almost invariably the rule for school.

Remarkable exceptions round the Mediterranean and Middle East Area are Iran (where the son of the Shah is left-handed, and allowed to sign visitors' books in public), Turkey, where Kemal Ataturk

changed the entire alphabet from arabic to roman in the nineteen-
twenties, and Israel which, with many different nationalities, allows
a complete freedom of choice. General Moshe Dayan has a left-
handed son. For the rest of the Muslim Middle East, the left hand is
especially tabu, as the unclean one. There are parts of Africa where
sinistral writing is grudgingly permitted (one of the sons of Chief
Enahoro of Nigeria is left-handed) and it is banned in most parts of
the Far East, with the exception of Japan.

Japanese script, however, starts at the top right-hand corner and
descends vertically to the bottom, continuing in a form like vertical
stripes. A "hidarikiki" (left-hander) does not find this as easy to do if
he is using the traditional brush. Once again, it is so easy to blot the
Nipponese copy book at the start as the left-handed brush is carried,
upward but laterally, across the page to the top right corner. True,
by the time a left-handed Japanese boy or girl is finishing the page,
on the left side, he is at an advantage: but with young people learning
to write, or slightly unsure of their ability, it is always the first few
words which are the hardest.

The Japanese brush, like the Chinese, produced graceful characters, like good italic script. But in the land which first produced the
felt-tipped pen (which dries at once and scarcely ever blots), such
writing is becoming increasingly rare.

It has always been a puzzle, both to experts and to laymen who
travel in the Middle East, to see Arabs and Jews, normally deadly
enemies over the centuries, share the habit of writing from right to
left, using the right. The proportion of left-handers, who are
encouraged to be sinistral, seems to be very high in Israel, abnormally
high for a Middle-Eastern country. Immigrants from Europe may
account partly for this, but among the native *sabras* and Israeli Arabs,
the same freedom holds.

Hebrew was once called "the left-handed language," but not,
apparently, because it was written with the left hand but because,
unlike the Greek and later the majority of languages, it travelled
towards the left. It is also likely that the actual flow of the Hebrew
characters favours a right to left movement.

This could be true of Arabic, but the Arab saying "It is better to
see where the pen is coming than not to see where it is going" puts
a different interpretation on it. Which is better, to risk hiding what

you have written, or to see it, as the western right-hander does?

There are indeed some left-handed Arabs who get away with it. One is no less distinguished than the Director of Tourism and Culture in the once traditional country of Libya. "*All* Arabs should write left-handed!" he declaimed to the author, scribbling that way in his office in Tripoli. Certainly the speed at which he performed his writing was considerable.

There may be yet another explanation of the right-left survival of Arabic and Hebrew (also Hindu and Japanese, which, though vertical, works its way anti-clockwise). The originators of joined-up letters, as distinct from single symbols, were probably the Phoenicians, writing from right to left. The Egyptians, with whom they traded, followed this pattern—and we must remember that the Hebrew Children of Israel were captives in Egypt for nearly twenty years, and must have picked up many of the characteristics of their captors.

The Greeks at first couldn't make up their minds. They tried right to left. Then a style known as "Boustrophedon," which curiously followed the movements of the plough, turning at the end of each furrow. This is a real collector's piece. Finally they came down on the left-right side, and since they founded the civilization of the western world, first the Romans (who had also accepted their formula for augury) then the others followed suit. Although Christian crusaders tried to conquer the Saracen infidel, their crusades made little impression. Therefore Arabs (and Turks at that time) did not come under the influence of the Greek-inspired way of life. Nor did the very considerable Roman colonies in North Africa though they were of a high civilization, and left many proud Latin inscriptions behind them in countries like Libya and Tunisia.

Mirror-writing, or reverse-image writing, is something which baffles right-handers, but it is well-known to many left-handers, the only ones who practise it. The artist Leonardo da Vinci wrote all his Notebooks in it: the Rev. C. L. Dodgson (Lewis Carroll) another primary left-hander, used it as a party trick for Alice and her friends.

Its origins, which are obscure, are first noted in the seventeenth century, and from time to time thereafter individual examples have appeared, though there has never been an "epidemic" involving a whole school of mirror-writers. J. K. Fuller, a Californian psychologist in the early twentieth century, ascribed it to a number of symptoms, such as physiological weakness through disease: weak-mindedness as a child: mere absent-mindedness: or simply, left-handedness. The former three could certainly not apply to Leonardo.

Certainly, as Dr. Margaret Clark points out, "for the left hand, the movement away from the body, the easier movement, is from right to left; thus if there is no inhibiting factor, either visual or intellectual, or if this is temporarily removed, the left hand may produce mirror-script. Mirror-writing is not a sign," she continues, "of mental deficiency, though its prolonged occurrence is common in mental defectives. . . . In short, though an intelligent left-handed child may produce mirrored letters or words in the early stages more frequently than does a right-handed child, visual clues and comparison with the writing in books will lead to the realization that his writing is somehow different and will suggest a correction to the tendency: but such a realization may not be present in a dull child."

Sir Cyril Burt, who has made a considerable study of the subject, adds a comment on another aspect—

"As the mirror-writer forms his letters, the correctness of the particular shapes and the wrongness of the general direction seem alike attributable to the fact that the nervous centres for motor control and the nervous centres for visual control may at times function in total independence. With nearly all of us, immediately an action becomes completely automatic, it tends to slip away from the control of the attentive eye, and to be left to the half-conscious guidance of the muscle sense."

Stopping "free" writing, and only allowing controlled writing following a copy may, in Dr. Clark's view, convert the persistent mirror-writer.

Are mirror-writers able to read their efforts? Dr. Macdonald Critchley wrote an entire book on the subject of mirror-writing, and gave his view on this particular point—

"The answer will depend on the particular type of patient concerned. In the case of the hemiplegic mirror-writer, it is probable that there is an inability to read both normal and reversed writing and indeed many such patients probably do not realize that their handwriting is in any way peculiar. Individuals with a congenital

Dextral watching a sinistral writing in train

type of mirror-writing—particularly when associated with left-handedness—probably cannot read their efforts at all. They will describe their mirror-writing as 'easy to do but very difficult to read.' In the case of the congenitally word-blind, however, reading is a matter of equal difficulty whichever direction the words are traced."

He adds this interesting remark: "For every right-handed defective who writes mirror-wise there are fifteen sinistrals. It has been stated that fifty per cent of a series of idiot children wrote mirror fashion, as contrasted with sixteen per cent of an identical number of normal controls." This test was made by Lochte.

There is another postscript on the general attitude of the young writer to the idea of the mirror image in writing.

"The child, in learning to write from left to right with his right hand is, as it were, unconsciously learning to write from right to left with his left hand . . . with the left hand, therefore, mirror-writing is a natural tendency to which we are all more or less liable; and our liability is greater, the more we are guided by the motor sense and the less we rely on vision. It is found most frequently of all among left-handed persons, because with them the left hand can execute fine movements with the greatest facility and consequently depends least on the guidance of the eye."

On the relationship of drawing and left-handedness, Sir Cyril Burt says in *The Backward Child*—

"I have noted how nearly 70 per cent of the human figures, drawn by children at the age of six, are shown full-face, and how, by the age of eleven, nearly 70 per cent are drawn in profile, facing (with right-handed children) to the left. But all parts of the body do not turn at the same stage or even in the same direction . . . The face may turn to the left, the feet perhaps to the right, while the trunk—and sometimes the eyes and mouth as well—are still displayed in full view. A child of normal intelligence soon perceives the inconsistency; but the dull often adhere to the same hybrid representation for a year or more. . . ."

"Much the same incongruities are to be seen in the efforts of primitive man: they appear in early Greek sculpture, and persist in Egyptian and Assyrian sculpture even down to the latest periods: here the head is always seen in profile, but the eye is in full face; the shoulders and body are seen from the front, and then, by a sudden twist, the legs and feet are drawn in profile. The lack of consistency arises from the fact that the child, like the primitive artist, disregards orientation and concentrates entirely on shape. . . ."

"It is instructive to note that, when a left-handed child draws a man's profile or a moving object like a railway train, he nearly always makes it face, not towards the left, as a right-handed child does, but towards the right. As anyone may prove to himself by outlining a forehead, nose and mouth, first with the right hand, then with the left, this principle yields the easiest movement in both cases. Further, in fitting on the hinder, and less important parts, the hand does not obscure what has already been drawn."

On the general subject of speech disorders leading to stammering and stuttering, a whole book could be written (and several have been produced, often with conflicting findings). We are concerned mainly with the relationship between stammering and handedness, but some definition and introduction is required also.

Ever since the days of Demosthenes, men have been concerned about fluency, or the lack of it, in speech. In an important debate at the senate in Rome Cicero once "stammered, blundered, and sat down" (Macaulay). Aristotle, Aesop, Virgil, King Charles I, King Louis II of France, Dean Swift, Dr. Johnson, Charles Lamb, Lewis Carroll, Charles Darwin, Walter Bagehot, Aneurin Bevan, Somerset Maugham—there is a long list of distinguished stammerers whose history of impediment is not so clearly chronicled as that of King George VI.

The word *stammer* is used in the Authorized Version of the Bible (Isaiah xxxii, 4) "The heart also of the rash shall understand knowledge, and the stammerer shall be ready to speak plainly."

Cyril Burt has discovered that Wyclif's translation of this word is *stuttynge*, and believes that this is about the first use of such a word. The German words *stammeln* and *stottern* have apparently much the same meaning. Burt also includes, in speech defects, *lalling* and lisping, concerning the mispronunciation of the letter *l* and the letter *s* respectively. (These are not primarily connected with handedness.) "Stammering," he adds, "should be distinguished from stuttering. Stuttering is the spasmodic repetition of speech: stammering is the spasmodic arrest of speech . . . the stutterer rhythmically re-commences; the stammerer silently sticks. The one says "bub-bub-bub-bub-butter!"; the other says nothing, and then burst out with a big "BUTter!" Of these two forms of hesitating speech, a simple stammer is by far the commoner: stuttering is much less prevalent in actual life than in anecdote or on the stage."

One might add that there are many in the professions of stage, radio, television and public speaking, who, while talking hesitatingly in private company, achieve complete fluency in public. The author has himself observed how Somerset Maugham, whose stutter was the bane of his private life, lost it entirely before the television cameras on first being interviewed in 1954 by Malcolm Muggeridge; none of his autobiographical works have hinted at his original sinistrality, but one would not be surprised to learn of it. Aneurin

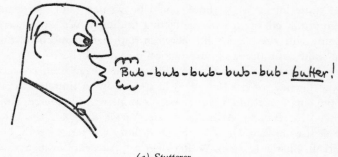

(a) Stutterer

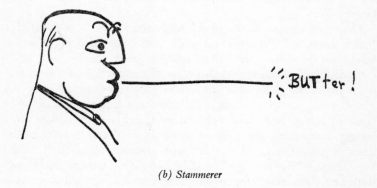

(b) Stammerer

Bevan made good use of his stammer in debates in the House of Commons. He was originally left-handed.

Burt's important London inquiry into backwardness in metropolitan schools revealed that those with severe speech defects were noted 1 per cent of the whole group, 5 per cent of the backward, and 15 per cent of the mentally defective. The main speech defect was stammering or stuttering. There have also been estimates of the whole population proportion in the following countries: U.S.S.R. 1·7 per cent, Germany 1·6 per cent, Belgium 1·4 per cent, Spain 1·2 per cent, Italy 1·0 per cent. He concludes that perhaps the more fluid quality of the Southern languages accounts for the lower estimate. Yet the figure given at the same time for the U.S. is only 0·87 per cent.

The American, Edward Travis, conducted an experiment in the 1930s with Dr. Bryng Bryngelson of Minnesota (the man whose own investigation into handedness revealed the startling contention that "If there were no interference on the part of parents and teachers, 34 per cent of all children born today would become left-handed"). Their report was remarkable enough: out of 200 stammering children, 62 per cent were "shifted" sinistrals, and Iowa University gave an average figure, over the years, of 43 per cent. "The acquired 'motor facility,' " Travis declared, "is out of harmony with the native psychological lead."

Burt's own figures for children of normal intelligence with speech-defects are as follows: 4·2 per cent left-handed and 6·1 per cent right-handed. "Thus the difference, though perceptible, is not very great; among left-handers who now habitually use the right hand, disturbances are less than half as common again. Now let us turn to the backward left-handers. Here the difference is far greater: stuttering is more than twice as common in those who have learnt to use the right. The percentages are 6·2 per cent and 13·9 per cent respectively."

He makes the point that the type of school makes a difference. In tolerant schools where left-handedness is allowed or even encouraged, the percentage is smaller. Where the rule-of-the-right is rigidly enforced, the number of stammerers goes up. "It is therefore difficult to withstand the inference that, in the main, it is the general severity of the school discipline—of which the insistence on right-handedness is but a sample—that is really responsible for an excess which appears equally in both the right-handed and left-handed groups."

But statistics about children are, by themselves, likely to be misleading. Many of the stammerers, both left- and right-handed, are likely to have been of a neurotic or emotionally unstable nature, and a lack of temperamental balance can of itself cause hesitation in speech through pure "nerves." Of children in London who, in 1911, were required to write with the right hand in a survey, 74 per cent showed no signs of stuttering, and later tests have supported this comparatively early examination.

Dr. Margaret Clark has given the question a thorough examination in recent years, which supports this early contention. Teachers and those in authority, she writes, have tended to return to their earlier policy of insistence on right-hand training. "They base their altered conduct on evidence which they claim reveals that actions performed with the left hand are less efficient than those with the right, and that it is consequently better for everyone concerned if all use the right hand. Their second justification is that changed handedness has no effect on speech. . . . It is probably true to say that this is a fairly accurate picture of the general attitude adopted today by many people in most countries. . . . Frequently the change is carried out before the child enters school." That is, by the parents, even after the child has entered school.

Who has formulated this theory?

Right-handers, of course. If they find no student-like rebellion against a peaceful conquest of others' sinistrality, they think it is all to the good. Authorities like this do not realize that, apart from the danger of speech disturbance, which is real in many cases, it is well-nigh impossible to convert a natural sinistral to perform *all* natural actions with the hand, foot or eye which is alien, even though victory may be won in the class-room.

Consider, then, the case of the "severe" school, perhaps not in Britain, the U.S., or Western Europe, but beyond the Iron Curtain, and in the Middle and Far East. Who knows in how many class-rooms the "odd child out," the *levja* in the Soviet Union, the *zurdo* in Spain, the *linkser* in Germany, the *canhoto* in Portugal, the *khabalabra* in India, the *stangaciu* in Rumania, the *levoruk* in Poland and Czechoslovakia, the *hidarikiki* in Japan—to name but a few in their own tongues—is made an object of odium by his teacher and ridicule by his schoolmates because he is left-handed and because his very name has a bad meaning? That there should be a world-wide universal law encouraging absolute freedom for left-handed writing in schools is, as we have tried to show, undeniable. Obviously there are many stammerers who are not "shifted" sinistrals, just as there are many right-handed school-children who are for other reasons the "odd child out." But since stammering can be such a nightmare existence for a child, just as it may be an almost intolerable handicap for an adult, anything that can be done to lessen the number of those with defects in speech should be encouraged.

The American therapist Van Riper was himself a cured stutterer.

Dr. Clark describes how his treatment of patients was to force them into positions which they had previously found difficult to assume, positions where they had to speak. He promised them support from as many devices as possible so that they could face the situation at a conscious level. His diagnosis according to Dr. Clark, was that "when the stutterer knew he had nothing to fear, and that he would no longer have to face the likelihood of appearing odd in the company of others, his personality underwent an apparently astonishing change. He was no longer a shy, inhibited introvert, since he now had the ability to enjoy social communication. It is a well-known fact that a number of great orators had some speech difficulties which they overcame, and having first mastered their handicap they used speech both as a means of social communication and of commanding power."

Tell that, one might have said, to King George VI, who received all the help his speech-therapist could give, but without the results quoted above.

Let us quote two more authorities. Abram Blau, the American who attributed to the sinistral almost every negative attitude in the book, described stuttering as "a symptom of psychoneurosis, with the pre-eminent role of the unconscious oral sadistic components in the symptom" (whatever that means). "In general, the neurosis has many obsessive-compulsive features. Like all neuroses, its origin must be sought in the early infantile and childhood history, centring around the emotional conflicts and antagonisms between child and parent."

We might agree that the stuttering child is shy and frightened. "He is a very insecure individual who is constantly in great emotional conflict." Blau links this disability with vomiting, bed-wetting, fussiness, fears, over-dependence on mother, and other neurotic symptoms, just as he linked left-handedness itself with a number of unpleasant traits, including constipation. But his main argument is that the stutterer is aggressive and hostile beneath it all. "Speech has many components and in stuttering its function as an agent for aggression is most prominent. In the unconscious of stutterers, speaking means mostly the utterance of 'bad' words, and an aggressive act, ultimately even a means of 'killing' with words. . . . Behind (the stutterer's) desire only to prove that he is right is concealed the utterly fantastic hostile tendency to destroy his opponents with words."

It may be recalled again that the sinistral, stuttering Mr. Aneurin Bevan used the delayed-action of words with great effect, particularly when attacking Mr. Winston Churchill, but this was achieved without the fluency which is supposed to come with confidence.

Well, the answer to speech difficulties, as with writing difficulties and sinistrality is, according to Professor Blau, in the negative. After reading his book *The Master Hand*, the sinistral might just as well regard himself as a second-class citizen. But Leonardo da Vinci and the others didn't, and "negative" left-handed types continue to perform astonishing feats of prowess in other fields.

The latest recruit to the theory that stammering has no link with handedness is Professor Wendell Johnson, speech pathologist at the University of Iowa's famous clinic, which has made many investigations into the subject with Dr. Bryng Bryngelson. His experience is related with typical good humour by Martin Gardner in his book *The Ambidextrous Universe*.

"Johnson himself stammered as a child, and there is a funny-sad section of his book (*Stuttering and What You Can Do about It*) in which he describes the succession of vain efforts to find a cure. He tried faith-healing, speaking with pebbles in his mouth" (the Demosthenes cure), "adjustments by a chiropractor, and three months in a stammering school where he swung dumb-bells while reciting such lines as 'Have more backbone and less wishbone.' He ended up at the University, where a new programme on stuttering was under way. The psychiatrists in charge were convinced that stuttering was related to handedness. There was no evidence whatever that Dr. Wendell Johnson was anything but strongly right-handed, but so well-anchored was the current theory that for ten years he tried to turn himself into a left-hander, without success! When the new data began to come out in the thirties, showing no correlation of stammering with handedness, Johnson himself could scarcely believe it."

The "new data" recommended trying gently to convert the sinistral child in writing and eating, unless he was determinedly left-handed. Fair enough, if done in an understanding way. But there

An authentic American badge

are many people today who, meeting a stammerer, find that he was originally a left-hander. Johnson continued—

"One of the theories current at the time of the first Study was that stuttering is caused by changing a left-handed child to right-handedness. It was also supposed by some authorities that more stutterers than non-stutterers were either left-handed or ambidextrous. This theory had been given its major support by the Iowa Speech Clinic in the 1920s and 1930s.

"One of the most important things we had learned from several laboratory studies was that the terms 'right-handed,' 'left-handed,' 'ambidextrous' and 'changed-handedness' were used in very different ways by different people—even by different clinicians and research workers.

"The basic fact is that normally each of us has two good hands, not just one . . . Most right-handed persons can, if necessary, learn to write and do other things also with the left hand, just as most left-handed persons can, if need be, get along quite well using the right hand."

This may be so, in a normal adult world, but Dr. Johnson's remarks do not so readily apply to the world of childhood and growing-up, where such adaptation on the part of the left-hander— it practically never happens in reverse for this is a right-handed world —can be not only very irksome but even frightening.

Dr. Johnson then refers to the "brain dominance" theory in general (the right side controlling the left hand, etc.) and adds: "The speculative part of the theory postulated that in the non-stutterer one side of the brain is somehow 'dominant over the other' and controls the discharge of nerve impulses from both sides of the brain so that the two sides of the body receive the same kind of impulse at the same time. This resulted, it was said, in the co-ordinated action of the muscles in normal speech. It was assumed that in stutterers neither side of the brain is dominant, so that the two sides act independently of each other, with the result that at any particular instant the two sides of the body may receive different kinds of nerve impulses."

This, it was thought, explained the action of the speech muscles in the case of the stutterer.

"It was," adds Johnson, "an assumption, a guess at what might be true. We do not have a standard definition of either 'brain dominance' or 'handedness.' There is no way to be sure, therefore, that 'handedness' is related to whatever anyone might intend to convey by 'the dominance of one side of the brain over the other' in the absence of clear specification of what is meant by both terms.

"We have already discussed the so-called handedness theory of stuttering. In view of the popularity this theory once enjoyed, it is of interest that the two groups of mothers and fathers made almost identical scores on our handedness questionnaires. The two groups of families (the control group and stutterers) were alike in handedness even when all blood relatives were included (the child's parents, brothers, and sisters, uncles, aunts and grandparents in each case). Children classified as stutterers, or their families, are not different from other people as far as handedness is concerned, according to our findings."

Tests for Left-handers

Importance of tests, especially for children—Necessity for wider tests in industrial life—The French Médecine de Travail *test of 1962 examined in detail—The London School of Economics test in 1946—Investigation into Ambiguous Handedness at London University—Investigation by Gesell and Ames (1947)—Sir Cyril Burt's report on backward children—Conclusions*

Tests for handedness and studies of left-handedness are common enough in Universities such as Iowa and London, and in experimental psychology and medical circles. These are mainly tests for children, and confine themselves to habits, prowess, speech and so on. What has been neglected in this right-handed world has been governmental inquiries into conditions for left-handers in industry. The right-handers, who dominate every sphere in the world (except sport) probably do not, for the most part, even know that such a problem exists. Factory owners and managers do not have the personal contact which a schoolmaster has with his class, nor have they the onus of seeing that any "problem" worker receives individual attention, as a teacher would on seeing a left-handed pupil in difficulties.

Such an investigation is badly needed in highly-industrialized countries such as Britain and the U.S., but practically nothing has been done. The efforts of Mr. William Gruby in London to jerk the elbows of manufacturers, pointing out the lack of household implements for left-handed use, has produced some useful results, but only with individual, small utensils. The largest is a Swedish left-handed work-bench. But, although many bench machines are adaptable to either hand, many are not, and the assumption by the right-hander is that the left-hander who cannot adapt himself and

"If you don't believe me—read this!"

"switch" hands should get out, and seek employment in which sinistrality is not a handicap. This attitude is no longer warrantable in an enlightened, inventive age. It is true, as the vast organization of IBM admits, that computer work and programming has perforce to be right-handed in design and operation, but for the ordinary workman with his vice or other implement on the bench, far too little attention has been paid, not only to the design, but the positioning of equipment. Even an automatic registry for filling-in bills has its perils for the sinistral if it is placed against a left-hand wall. The author recalls that, in his first job in an advertising agency in London, junior staff had to sign in by pulling a lever on the *right* side of the machine, which revealed a paper space marked with the time. Since it was fixed close against the left-hand wall, it was almost impossible for a left-hander to sign at all. When this fact was brought to the attention of the management, it was dismissed as "frivolous," although quite a large proportion of the staff, including copywriters, secretaries, and in particular, graphic artists, were left-handed. The author risked being dismissed by refusing to sign. The machine was never detached from the wall.

If one of the chief executives had himself been left-handed, of course, this "key-to-the-door" between members of a sinistral "freemasonry" would have aroused interest. Left-handers always stick together, except when they are rivals on the sports field. There is a common bond among the deprived minority, often derided at school and neglected in their manipulative work.

The most remarkable governmental test on handedness seems to have taken place in Hungary in the 1930s. It was scheduled to last eight years, but probably World War II intervened, and it is very hard to find anything but odd, fragmentary results. The really ambitious effort was launched by the French in 1962, the *Médecine de Travail*, with full French ministerial and medical patronage, participants from half-a-dozen countries, and the blessing of such well-known industrial firms as Esso, Gaz de France, French Railways, Shell, Renault, and others. The President of the Committee was Professor H. Desoille. The investigation was carried out by four Frenchmen, under the direction of M. Christiaens, of Lille.

The committee, in their long report of 1962, declare in their introduction that part of the investigation was to distinguish, among selected groups of French workmen, not only between left-handed and right-handed, but also between direct left-handedness and "contrary left-handedness." Far too little attention had been paid, they said, to the hand-problems of French manual workers, of whom at least a million and a half were known to be *gauchers*.

The introduction goes into the whole question of laterality, dominant hemispheres, and the other neurological theories of handedness which are common to any full-scale examination of the subject. On the question of left-handedness in families they have some interesting statistics. Two right-handed parents will produce, on average, 2·1 per cent left-handers. One right-handed, one left-handed parent produce 17·3 per cent left-handers, and two left-handed parents, 46 per cent left-handers. These are very high figures in comparison with some other reports. Their view about dominant or recessive heredity is guarded, and neutral.

It would be simple, the committee points out, if mankind could be divided into natural right-handers and left-handers—but it isn't as simple as all that. One cannot make out a proper balance-sheet and expect everyone to conform to it. There are the intermediate cases which may show incomplete lateralization, and deny the previous theory of crossed laterality. (This is all in keeping with the latest pronouncements of Zangwill and Wendell Johnson.)

They therefore had in mind the following considerations—

1. A pathological "asymmetry" within left-handedness;
2. Neurological symptoms associated with *gaucherie*; these symptoms are well-known, and common to many left-handers who cannot easily adapt themselves to the practices of the majority.

The questionnaires followed the usual pattern, and were mainly concerned with the dominant hand for deliberate actions such as writing, with instinctive actions such as catching a ball, wielding a tennis-racket, cutting with scissors, kicking a football, and shooting with a rifle; they ended with questions about any troubles with speech and stammering during childhood, and particular hindrances at work.

The questionnaire also asked whether the subject had been forced to become right-handed when young, and whether he had difficulty in distinguishing between right and left in giving traffic instructions. There was a second separate inquiry among doctors, dentists and musicians, which included the use of instruments and the degree of ambidextrality which might arise in their work. A third group consisted of over 1,000 miners and metal workers from the Bassin du Nord. Additional questions to them included: striking a match, dealing cards, looking through a key-hole, mounting a bicycle, kneeling at the rock-face, and the preferred foot in childhood at the French version of hop-scotch (*marelle*).

The results came out as follows (it is only possible to give general statistics, but the French team produced a very closely detailed report covering every branch of this particular investigation). Of the men (784 candidates) the number of left-handers and partially left-handed came to 88, or 11·2 per cent of the total. Of the women

(396 candidates) 36 were left-handed, or 9·1 per cent of the total·
There was also an eye-test: 14 per cent of right-handed men were
left-eyed, and 21 per cent of women; 34 per cent of left-handed men
were right-eyed, and 19 per cent of women. This would argue a
great diversity in eye dominance.

Tests were also made on the same group about speech defects and
stammering. Out of 696 right-handers, men, 31 stammered (4·4 per
cent) and out of 88 left-handers, 6 stammered (6·7 per cent). Figures
for women were much lower for both hands, and the conclusion
was reached that there was no direct connection between laterality
and stammering. But on a separate test of 100 juvenile delinquents,
15 per cent of left-handers were found to have speech defects, as
against 4·5 per cent of right-handers—a small but significant sample.

Hand-ability among 25 left-handers was then studied, and *valeur
générale*, and their general rating was *médiocre*. Shorthand-writing
then followed with 32 stenographers from the Post Office and 12
teenagers. Best speeds from left-handers were 14 per cent, low
speeds 20 per cent. Right-handers romped home with 89 per cent
best speeds. It seems that the left-handed *sténo-dactylo* is not as
efficient in France as she is in England or the United States.

We move on now to *Industries de la confection* (in this case, ready-
made clothes). Here the 965 workers were mainly women, and the
number of left-handers negligible at 3·4 per cent, although further
investigation, says the report, would probably have produced a
higher proportion. On examination, the left-handers in the various
departments of clothing factories seem to have given every satisfac-
tion. Much of the machinery was for bi-manual use, particularly in
the sewing departments, where electric pedal operation was available
for *les gauchers*. Left-handed garment cutters were provided throughout with sinistral scissors. "Pas de problème" was the summing-up
of the head of the inquiry, M. Bize.

The investigation covered a wide range of industries exhaustively:
it is possible only to summarize the various findings.

In a washing-machine factory certain difficulties in operation by
the 8 per cent of left-handers were observed, but an equal number
of difficulties were experienced by right-handers. There was no
hesitation in accepting left-handed applicants for jobs.

In the department of *Postes et Télégraphes* certain operations have to be made with the right hand (or finger, on the dial) although switchboard operation is bi-manual. Left-handers in the Paris *Interurbain* office seem to be very adaptable to certain dextral usages. In telephone boxes, of course, the French notice the same problem obtaining in Britain and many other countries: the difficulty a left-hander has (with the apparatus on the left) in writing down a message quickly. But there is no ban on employing left-handers at *Postes et Télégraphes* offices and exchanges. The difficulties have been noted.

After investigating a construction works in Alsace, this report actually concludes that, among 2,500 employees, the left-hander, or at least the ambidextral, is at an advantage in operating the machines. The point is made that a left-hander's operations with the right hand are more assured and accurate than a right-hander's with the left hand, sinistrals being more adaptable. The accident possibilities seem also to be lower among left-handers, and this particular management has been considering training its right-handed staff in the improved use of the *left* hand—quite a revolution in its way!

The same conclusion seems to have been reached in the spinning-mill of Amédée Prouvot. Left-handers here, though only a small minority, are highly esteemed for their bi-manual skill. "Pas de problème" is again the message from the Cadum–Palmolive soap factory, and one foreman employs a left-hander to wield a hammer for a certain job which a right-hander cannot do. Eleven left-handers in a paper mill all have high efficiency records, and can work the machinery well. So the fascinating and painstaking record goes on: 10 per cent of left-handers at a big *bonneterie* making hosiery: Otis elevator-manufacturers requiring left-handers in some cases acquire ambidextrals: 10 per cent of left-handed pupils at *Une Ecole des Métiers Féminins* (a sort of business training-school which included clothing, modelling, hairdressing and the like: some pupils had to be given special instruction, or were advised to try and use both hands equally, in which case they proved to be excellent trainees).

Finally, M. Christiaens himself, helped by M. Bize, conducted a study on doctors, dentists and musicians. General statistics out of the sample: 9 per cent of doctors (out of 152), 13·7 per cent of dentists (out of 162), violinists 8 per cent and pianists 10 per cent (for them the handicap is non-existent). With doctors, the instruments can largely be used equally well with the left hand, or ambidextrally

Forever Ambi. The dream of the
Ambidextral Culture Society, 1905

(the ambidextral doctor has always had a considerable advantage over his one-handed colleagues). The difficulty arises, says the report, in training, when the left-hander has to "re-translate" all that he has been taught in manual methods.

M. Christiaens then sums up the results of his inquiries into the workers in the *Houillères Nationales*—the coal-miners of the north. On an average, 7·5 per cent of them are left-handed, but he finds no particular problems facing them, and no increase in the accident rate for left-handers. Among trainee-miners the proportion of *gauchers* is higher—9 per cent. After an examination of workers at the coal-face itself, the conclusion is that the left-hander is able to work the automatic machinery without much difficulty, even if the indicators are on the wrong side.

The inquiry then moved to left-handed bus drivers and conductors, and concludes that there is not much of a problem here, and no refusal to employ left-handers. Indeed, the accident-rate seems almost equally divided in a survey of the bus-service in the Toulouse area, between the *droitiers* and the *gauchers*. If anything with a percentage of 0.88 against 1.20, the left-handers seem, in proportion, to be more careful.

"It is surprising," M. Christiaens continues, "that we cannot find a connection between sinistrality and 'behaviour-troubles' in factories. This has nothing to do with handwriting or speech-troubles. There are obviously people with a stammer, who are dyslexic, who are rebels, who lack a social sense, who are lacking in any impulsive sense. But a normal left-hander, in most jobs, presents no more problems than a normal right-hander. Indeed, in precision jobs which require delicate usage, the man who can alternately use, with skill, the left hand and the right hand, is of great value."

Moreover, he adds, the left-hander is usually aware of his left-handedness, and therefore more willing to try and adapt himself to bi-manual usage, thus becoming a more useful member of the community. In the more highly developed professions, such as that of surgery, the left-hander with an ability occasionally to work right-handed is at a distinct advantage. With those who experience difficulty in manual operations, he adds, it may not be their left-handedness itself which is the main cause of the trouble.

"Le sujet par exemple est maladroit, ou bègue [stammering] ou d'un caractère difficile, *et* il est gaucher: rien ne nous prouve qu'il le soit *parce qu'il* est gaucher." Many right-handers seen during the investigation have similar retarding factors which are nothing to do with handedness.

M. Christiaens then deals with the problem of the "switched" left-hander, *le gaucher contrarié*. These are the problem cases, and he cites the usual ritual of being mocked at in childhood, being forcibly converted to the right with a degree of brutality, and being forced to keep up with the speed of the rest of the class—treatment familiar to many a left-hander throughout the world. The general statistic ranges, within the scope of the whole examination, between 5 per cent and 20 per cent of left-handers.

If there were no stigma attached to left-handedness, he argues, all might be well, and on the practical side he comes down on the

side of those who believe in "switching" a left-hander, painlessly
and early in life ("pas d'interdictions brutales, pas de 'tabous,' pas de
'la belle main,' pas de moqueries ni d'humiliation à l'âge tendre").
Above all, even if it is deemed correct to bring up a *gaucher* left-
handedly, as far as writing and manual actions are concerned, there
must be no suggestion of inferiority for the person concerned.

Finally, M. Christiaens, after what must be the most exhaustive
and detailed examination into left-handedness conducted in Europe
in recent years, comes to his conclusions. Thousands of workers have
been watched, in dozens of professions, "avec une égale rigueur
objective."

What, then, are the conclusions?

First, that left-handers in French industry offer no outstanding
problems in safety, hygiene, adaptation or absenteeism, and that
their special requirements as left-handers are widely realized in the
various trades.

There remain, first, jobs for which left-handers are not suitable,
particularly in the garment and metal-trades, but here again,
machinery could be easily adapted to suit the left-hander or the
ambidextral. With about a million left-handers in industry, this
would be worth doing. Left-handed dentists' chairs form a special
plea by M. Christiaens, even if, as he says, their construction provides
certain difficulties—as indeed it probably does.

"Once the left-handed apprentice has overcome his first difficulties," says M. Christiaens, "his adaptation provides excellent
results, and the left-handed worker is 'integrated' into his company
with very satisfactory results." He recommends that in big com-
panies, a left-hander should be appointed to what is called *le Comité
d'Hygiène et de Sécurité*.

"It must be noted," add the two reporters, "that among the
twenty left-handed doctors revealed by the inquiry, many were
found to be eminent *maîtres*—masters of their profession—in the
hospitals of Paris and the provinces."

Dentists experienced trouble only in the position of the instruments,
the dental chair itself, and the spittoon for the patient. The report
adds that left-handed dental chairs can be found in the United States.

As far as musicians are concerned, the reporters are obviously
aware of the piano concertos for the left-hand only, notably that

of the Basque composer Maurice Ravel, written for his friend Paul Wittgenstein, whose right hand was injured in the First World War. There is a hint that Chopin, whose piano works emphasize the power of the right hand, was originally a left-hander. With the organ there is "pas de problème." Two hands, two feet, two eyes—it is a bimanual operation if ever there was one.

Among violinists, every solo player would claim that the hand that wields the bow provides the most sensitive part of playing— *l'âme du violon.* The inquiry has not been carried much further: if so, it would have revealed just what changes are necessary in the instrument, and how impossible it is for the left-hander to take part in an orchestra.

As will be realized, this inquiry by the French *Médecine de Travail* is a sensitive as well as a detailed one. Over and over again the point is made that left-handers who have acquired a certain dextral skill can be the most useful workers of all. Right-handers, he claims, do not properly realize, fortified as they are by tradition, language and custom, the value of left-hand usage. It is in the interplay of the two hands that the best work lies, not in the dominance of the one over the other. "Nos mains ont tendance à travailler en symmétrie, l'éducation doit viser à leur donner une orientation parallèle. . . . Il y a une mine pour l'éducation gestuelle," he concludes, and adds a strong recommendation to the right-hander to develop skill in his left hand. "Contrariwise," as Tweedledee put it in *Alice Through the Looking-glass,* the obstinate, determined left-hander is equally at fault. He must become *un gaucher éduqué,* one who realizes the value of a two-handed operation. The fault lies in thinking of one-handedness. The future for left-handers is to adapt themselves. "Man thinks with his muscles," he adds. Therefore he should think with both, not with one alone. This is the main conclusion of an investigation which has covered an entire field of manual activity, and one which could well be carried out in other countries.

A National Survey Sample was held among 5,362 children born in Great Britain during the first week of March, 1946. The report on this came from the Medical Research Unit of the London School of

Economics (J. W. B. Douglas, J. M. Ross and J. E. Cooper). "The hand and eye preferences . . . are related," runs the introduction, "to educational ability and attainment, emotional adjustment and speech defects." As it is based on a representative sample at normal schools, this study is not open to the selective bases that are likely to occur in studies of clinic populations.

The first examination was made by school doctors of children between the ages of 6 and 11. It was found that 10 per cent of both boys and girls were inconsistent in their hand preferences: 7 per cent of boys and 5 per cent of girls were consistently left-handed. When the division was made between middle and manual working class, the percentage went up one per cent among the boys, and down one per cent among the girls (probably, one suspects, due to home influence by the mother). Quoting the findings of Burt and Zang-will, the investigators recommended a painless transference to right-handedness at a very early stage. "The pressure to use the right hand should be stage-managed so that the right hand is adopted naturally and mechanically."

Although not all the children examined in 1946 were available, at a later age, for a second test in 1961, there were sufficient to give adequate division into Known Hand Preferences and Unknown Hand Preferences, the proportion being roughly 50-50, between the ages of 8 and 15. There followed a series of test scores related to ability and attainment, and here, on the aggregate number, there was little difference between pronounced left- and right-handers, but a slight reduction on the "inconsistent" group.

For the 15-year-olds, the test scores were divided into speech, mathematics, and reading, and the results are very heartening for the left-handers, who were above the average in the last two categories. The poorest readers were those with inconsistent hand-preference. "Of 367 children, 27 were regarded by their teachers as being out-standingly bad readers as compared with an expected 20. This excess is explained for the most part by the relatively high proportion of manual working class children who are ambidextrous."

Those who were changed, between the ages of 8 and 15, in writing from left to right hand, or, more rarely, switched back from right to left, show no significant difference in their test scores, but the examiners add: "perhaps those who changed from their right to

Ocular Dominance

their left hand were really reverting to their preferred hand, and, after giving a slightly depressed score at 8 (48 per cent) were subsequently able to redeem themselves (50·18 per cent at 15 years). Alternatively, those who changed from their left to their right hand were forced to use their non-dominant hand and this resulted in a relative deterioration in test performance during the school years (44·88 per cent at 15 years)."

With regard to emotional adjustment, the report says: "children who are inconsistent in their hand preferences are said to be more often emotionally disturbed, and are more likely to stammer than children who are consistently right- or consistently left-handed. Further it has been suggested that children who are ambidextrous have difficulties at school which produce stress situations followed by anxiety and a variety of symptoms of emotional disturbance such as night-terrors, truancy and pilfering. It has also been said that half of all stutterers are ambidextrous, and that when stuttering occurs in a left-handed child who has been forced to use his right hand, a return to left-handedness often produces a great improvement." (This theory is certainly borne out in correspondence received by the Left-Handers' Association.)

The report then deals with eye-dominance among the school sample, and comes to the conclusion that children who sight with their right eye (as do most right-handers) do better in the tests than those who prefer the left eye, particularly in the later age groups of 11 and 15, and particularly with the manual working class, who at 15 are probably already destined for a trade which will involve hand-preference in a factory, or shop, or office.

An investigation into aspects of Ambiguous Handedness was made by Mrs. Sankya Naidoo, now psychologist at the Word Blindness Centre for Dyslexic Children, Coram Fields, London, as a thesis for the University of London in 1961. It was concerned mainly with children who exhibit a lack of unilateral handedness. Over 400 children were examined, from which twenty were selected, matched for sex, age and school (between four years nine months and five years eleven months). They were in turn matched with twenty strongly right-handed and twenty strongly left-handed children. Investigation was made into manual motor skill, speech development, present articulation of speech, sound discrimination, visual perception and family history.

There was found to be a greater difference in performance between the right-handed and ambiguously handed, who exhibited lower level of performance—but less difference between these ambiguously handed and sinistrals than between the dextrals and sinistrals.

There were ten tests given to 418 children, which might serve as a pattern for anyone attempting such an examination: block building; cutting with a knife; threading a needle; folding arms; drawing; putting incense sticks in a holder; cutting with scissors; hammering; throwing; finger painting.

Among the results, outstanding examples were—

Knife-cutting	Boys 89·1% right	10·5% left	4·0% either
	Girls 89·0% right	11·0% left	nil either
Drawing	Boys 90·3% right	8·8% left	0·8% either
	Girls 87·0% right	13·0% left	nil either
Putting sticks	Boys 62·0% right	7·5% left	30·0% either
	Girls 70·0% right	9·5% left	20·0% either
Folding arms	Boys 39·5% right	60·0% left	0·5% either
	Girls 44·0% right	55·4% left	0·5% either

This is only a sample of Mrs. Naidoo's preliminary investigation, but it shows a wide disparity, particularly between the more intricate and the easier actions, in which the left-handers are in a high proportion. A total count of threading a needle is—

50·8% right; 21·7% left; 27·5% either

But by contrast, cutting with scissors—

90·8% right;   9·2% left; nil either

(The last-named is presumably a semi-expert act, dictated by the influence of parent or teacher, but in the absence, presumably, of left-handed scissors now available.)

Mrs. Naidoo's test, therefore, reveals much more bilaterality in block building, threading a needle, and putting sticks in a holder, the first and third of these becoming somewhat similar activities. Folding of arms was not regarded as a sufficiently decisive proof. (It can be applied to crossing legs and clapping hands, but much depends on whether the child concerned is on its own, and free to use either action instinctively—there is no such concentration of effort as there is in, say, cutting with scissors or writing.)

The distribution of handedness was as follows—

Strong right	Boys 76·5%	Girls 82·6%
Weak right	8·9%	4·5%
Ambiguous	6·6%	2·3%
Weak left	1·7%	1·7%
Strong left	6·3%	8·9%

"It is suggested," Mrs. Naidoo adds, "that the almost equal numbers of left-handed boys and girls found in this investigation may be a reflection not only of different social attitudes to left-handedness today but also to the general greater permissiveness towards children nowadays."

On the family side, it was found that fourteen of the twenty left-handed children were *second* children.

On tests in motor skill, the dextrals performed more efficiently with their right hand than either the sinistrals or the ambiguous when using their own preferred hand. With the right-handed, the dominant hand was appreciably the more skilful, more so than with the left-handed. So were the right-handers appreciably superior to both the other groups in tests of hand and eye co-ordination and motor control. (Not much comfort here for sinistral children!)

A. Gesell and A. B. Ames (1947) made a study of the development of handedness in children between eight weeks and ten years. Examination revealed marked shifts in handedness even when dominance was established, the most frequent being a shifting in the first year of life. Here is a summary, a useful guide to those with young children—

12–20 weeks	Contact unilateral and generally with the left hand
24 weeks	Definite shift to bilaterality
28 weeks	Shift to unilaterality
32 weeks	Shift to bilaterality
36 weeks	Greater unilaterality with left predominating
40–44 weeks	Usually right or left, with right predominating
48 weeks	In some a temporary and in many a last shift to the use of one hand or the other
52–56 weeks	Shift to clear unilateral dominance of right hand
80 weeks	Much bilaterality and use of non-dominant hand
2 years	Relatively clear-cut unilateral use of right hand
2½–3½ years	Marked shift to bilaterality
4–6 years	Unilaterality—right hand predominating
7 years	Last period when left hand or both hands bilaterally used
8 years plus	Unilaterality

Sir Cyril Burt, the great authority on mentally handicapped children, carried out an experiment, when he held the post of Psychologist to the London County Council, with 5,000 boys and girls. He tested them individually in many habitual actions such as using a pencil, cutting with scissors, hammering, picking up marbles, stirring with a teaspoon, and so on. Here is his table of results—

INCIDENCE OF LEFT-HANDEDNESS AMONG
NORMAL, BACKWARD AND DEFECTIVE CHILDREN

	Ordinary Elementary Schools		Special Medical Defective Schools
	Normal	*Backward*	*Defective*
Boys	5·8%	9·6%	13·5%
Girls	3·7%	6·0%	10·3%
Average	4·8%	7·8%	11·9%

From this, Burt deduced, naturally, that the proportion of defective left-handers was very high, but held that the reason was mainly psychological, not physical: that, in other words, the left-hander was often the "odd boy out," and subject, not only to disapproval by a traditional teacher, but to the heartless persecution which has so often gone on in schools.

"The connexion between left-handedness and inferior intelligence" Burt writes, "is by no means close or regular. Among bright and imaginative children, left-handedness is far from rare; and biographers report many eminent persons, of high ability and unquestioned skill, as having been left-handed."

He then quotes some of the famous names mentioned in this book, describing some, like Leonardo and Michelangelo and many well-known surgeons today, as ambidextrous. He concludes: "Many of the dull and backward who pass for left-handed may truthfully be designated ambi-sinistral; they seem not so much dextrous with the left-hand as *gauche* with the right . . . ." Indeed, if it is ever safe to treat left-handedness as a sign or symbol, it should be regarded rather as a mark of an ill-organized nervous system than of a dull or deficient mind.

There are many other examples of tests being made in various countries, with the object of helping as well as merely classifying the left-hander. Professor Zangwill of Cambridge has made a valuable contribution to our knowledge of cerebral dominance by a prolonged study of brain-damage cases. Recently a survey was started by the Department of Psychology at Hull University. In Oxford, a Harvard researcher, Dr. Drewson, is conducting experiments on speech therapy with animals, particularly the monkey, at

5

the Department of Experimental Psychology, and there is evidence that a number of students, given a choice of subjects for their preliminary thesis, are choosing left-handedness. It is, indeed, a subject which is attracting a growing interest—and deservedly so.

An attempt to get Government support for an inquiry similar to the one in France met with failure in the House of Commons in May 1969, when Mr. Gwilym Roberts, M.P. for South Bedford (and himself a right-hander), put the following question to the then Secretary of State for Employment and Productivity—

"What she estimates to be the number of employed people who are left-handed: if she will publish in the official report any available breakdown; and if she will initiate an investigation into the increase in productivity which may be achieved by introducing left-handed working arrangements for left-handed people."

He got a dusty answer indeed from Mrs. Barbara Castle—or rather from her deputy, who saw no purpose in initiating such an inquiry; could not supply any statistics; erroneously stated that the percentage of left-handers was five; and ended loftily that "most left-handed people satisfactorily adapt themselves to existing machinery and plant lay-out."

There the matter unfortunately rests. Note that what Mr. Roberts was asking for was not that machinery should be specially constructed for left-handed workers, but that "working arrangements" could be adapted. There are firms which do this, and which recognize that many sinistral workers have genuine difficulty in handling their machines. The accident rate, one estimate has said, is about 30 per cent higher among left-handed workers, which speaks for itself.

It's yet another example of the right-hander not knowing what the left-hander is doing—and not caring.

"Let not your left brain know
what your right brain is doing" (Bernard Shaw)

Case Histories from Correspondents

Extracts from letters to the Left-Handers' Association—A cri-de-cœur from South Arabia—A rebel in Massachusetts—Stammering problems—Children's education and handedness—Handwriting—Shorthand—Politics—Hockey—Dentistry—The Zodiac—Household gadgets—A protest from Australia

*A*re left-handers conscious of being left-handed? Members of the Left-Handers' Association come from many countries, including the United States, Canada, France, Holland, Eire, Denmark, Israel, Czechoslovakia, Germany, Australia, New Zealand, Rhodesia, Morocco, Libya, Italy, Cyprus, Nigeria, South Arabia (Aden), Senegal, Gibraltar, Rumania and Hong Kong.

Many of them merely express general interest in the subject, and recount some minor experience of their own sinistrality. Some discount the whole idea that left-handedness is a handicap, and say they've not even thought twice about it (they obviously have not wrestled with a right-handed tin-opener!) but the trials and tribulations of the majority form an interesting comment on the position of the left-handed minority throughout the world. The extracts which follow are individual case-histories which, if a world-wide investigation were made, would be reflected in many more countries, since the handicaps follow a pattern in everyday life, in the classroom, the kitchen, in higher education, and in society, which is common among mankind.

A typical *cri-de-cœur* comes from a lady in a trouble-spot, in South Arabia, at El Inihad: "For many years I have seethed with indignation

"The stranger greets thy hand with proffered left?
Accept not; 'tis of loyalty bereft" (Harvey)

at the attitude of the general public towards left-handedness and composed (in my head) countless letters to the newspapers, to have such words as 'sinister' and 'gauche' expunged from the English language, to which, in the first place, they don't belong.

"Here, in Arabia, there is not the same stigma attached to a left-handed child—perhaps it is more natural, as they write from right to left! But it is insulting to eat with the left hand; however, I think this may well relate to a very real fear on the part of the host that the right hand was toying with a dagger."

It may also relate to the Unclean Hand, which is still a very real factor with the Muslim attitude to life. On the general situation, a resident of Windsor has this to say: "I do not think right-handed people realize at all how extensive is the right-handedness of the world they have made for themselves and consequently how adaptable left-handed people have to be to live in it."

Another rebellious attitude is expressed in this letter from a lady in Arlington, Massachusetts: "I have spent my whole life (62 years) arguing and fighting with right-handed people.

"I think the most important action *is to educate right-handed people that they aren't correct,* they are only a majority.

"My parents let nature take its course and my father prepared me psychologically by telling me that *convention isn't always right.*

"I only had trouble with one teacher and all she asked was that I should hold my pencil and paper in the same position as the right-handed children, I told her, point blank, 'I won't.' She bided her time until she could send me to the principal and call me insubordinate.

"I am a garment stitcher. I've had quite a few arguments with my co-workers because *I make them nervous by the way I handle my work.* My foreladies have called me stubborn. I've had can-openers and knives wrest from my hand, only because I turn them in the opposite direction. The person who does this, doesn't realize the dangers of such an action; either one could be accidentally stabbed. I tell them, 'if I make you nervous—don't watch me.' "

This pugnacious attitude is worthy of a Daughter of the American Republic. Since there is a Left-Handed Society in Arlington Street, Illinois, perhaps the writer has already joined—as a fighting member!

Although the problem of stammering is dealt with fully elsewhere in this book a large number of letters are concerned with this disability, which many still believe—and may well have good cause to believe—is caused by the compulsory "switching" of hand-preference at home or at school. From Bradford: "You will not object that I write right-handed. This was forced on me at school. Up to the time of leaving I had a stammer, but when I was able to develop my natural instinct, it left me."

This letter was received from a man in Chadwell Heath, near London: "For 65 years I have been left-handed, awkward, and clumsy! Recently I taught myself to write with my right hand, and although it is more legible and pleasing to the eye, it is a lengthy, laborious task, and moreover, a physical strain. All my life I have stammered, a common trait among left-handers. Incidentally, I have always enjoyed wonderful health, both physical and mental. Should I give up all attempts to write with my right hand, which is both neat and clear—or should I revert to my left-handed style, which is not so legible?"

It is not an easy question to answer.

A correspondent in Leicester writes: "I am a 'cack-handed' business woman and housewife. I run a small business of my own and look after my family. The youngest of my children, age 17 and 13, are left-handed. Many people might say that my teaching made them left-handed, but this was not so, as from infancy I tried to encourage them to use the right hand, but both of them found it more natural to use the left.

"When my son was ten years old, a teacher at school tried to make him use his right hand. I was not aware of this for some time, only that he was nervy, developed a stammer, was not eating or sleeping properly and was losing weight.

"Not until I sought the help of a psychologist did I realize the reason for his odd behaviour, and when protest was made to the school, his behaviour returned to normal. The following year he obtained a place in a grammar school, and took his 'O' level exams last year.

"As a child, I was the only left-hander in the family, and I well remember my mother, on my first day at school, clearly stating to the teacher that on no account was I to be made to use my right hand. I never was! But being left-handed tends to make one more adaptable, and one has to learn to be partly ambidextral in a right-handed world."

Many of the letters concern handwriting, as one would suppose: here is one from Kent.

"As a child I could only do and understand mirror-writing and therefore did not learn to read until much later than my contemporaries, and my left-handedness caused many difficulties during my education. I could not play tennis against anyone but another left-hander, and a few weeks before I sat for an examination I was informed that I would have to get a left-handed pen, so that my writing might be understandable. The local stationers were unable to obtain such a nib for at least three months, but I still managed to pass the examination."

Pen-nibs for left-handers are now, fortunately, easy to obtain, from a cheap pen for children to a classic pen which will last for life. Obviously the arrival of the ball-point and later the felt- and the plastic-tipped pen have made life easier for the left-handed writer. No more smudged copy-books. But it is handwriting without character, and anyone who cares about the formation of letters in an artistic way will always demand a true italic nib. Now, this is possible, at last.

In addition to handwriting, shorthand seems to provide a problem for left-handers, although the Perfect Secretary for Britain in 1965, chosen by the London Chamber of Commerce, was left-handed Mrs. Nancy Hall of Wimbledon, who averaged 130 words per minute, and experienced no trouble. Different is this experience from Torquay, Devon: "In the 1930s when employment was difficult, I applied for a post as shorthand typist, and instead was offered the only vacancy, that of addressograph operator, which I would have taken temporarily, but on being shown the mechanism, I was turned down, as it was possible only for a right-handed operator . . . ."

Others have written explaining the difficulties of learning shorthand: "The crucial test was to whether the strokes were made correctly to make up a word. My wrist, of course, was articulated in the wrong direction." This woman correspondent from Sheffield adds: "My husband teases me because I belong to three downtrodden minorities—women, left-handers and Jews. So it's nice to know that I have the chance to become less downtrodden in at least one respect!"

Here is a political note from a correspondent in Sussex, who has been examining the Left Bank in Paris: "The *Ile de la Cité* is *le bateau de Paris*, the original city, and it faces Westwards. The prow of the 'boat' points seawards, therefore the *rive gauche* is on the south side. There is nothing political about it. The early inhabitants probably knew right from left better than north from south, and the definition stuck."

Politically, however, the phrase "The Left" in parliamentary history, also came from Paris. In 1789, when the revolutionary Commune was formed, this opposition group sat on the left of the speaker in the *Chambre des Députés* (as does the opposition in Britain's Houses of Parliament).

The phrase "left-wing" applying to Socialists, has been traced back to a more recent date: the revolutionary German sailors at the end of the First World War, in Kiel.

But when there is a Socialist majority, then the left-wingers sit on the right, on Government Benches, and the right-wingers sit on the left, which is all mildly confusing, but may well be based on the arrogant assumption by right-wingers that the left-wing, like the left hand, would always be in a minority.

Another left-hander from London writes: "We can band together to stick up for our 'rights.' As a journalist, I find people say they can recognize my left-handed 'ticks,' because they go backwards: others say my writing slopes upwards: so I have to retaliate by saying that any fool can write with his right hand, and it takes brains to use one's left—and upward writing is a sign of optimism!"

Most parents are concerned about their children. A typical comment comes from another London district: "My daughter aged 18 is completely left-handed, and as she is due to start her nurse training, I hope she doesn't run into too many difficulties (I am myself ambidextral, and a trained nurse, so I find this very convenient). She has overcome many difficulties at school, even learning to play the trumpet, which is built for right-handed players, but although she looks most awkward when holding it, she plays well. She was unable to play hockey at school, as no one could produce a left-handed hockey-stick, and she just could not cope with the normal one."

No wonder, there isn't such a thing as a sinistral stick for hockey. Perhaps your daughter should try ice-hockey. In that game it's permissible.

A cheerful report comes from a correspondent in Bratton, Wiltshire, who, like a number of others, had to change hands, owing to a stroke.

"I was *very* right-handed, and it was terribly difficult to change to the left at over sixty, especially as I am now one-handed. I am telling you this because I want you to realize that being naturally left-handed *can* be an advantage. Most left-handed people learn to use their right hand for some things, but how many complacent right-handers trouble to use their left hand? I was a trained teacher, dealing with children from four to eleven. Usually about a quarter to a third of any group were found to be left-handed. I have never forced them to use their right hand. Usually I have said, 'Oh, you are lucky. You will naturally have to use your right hand for some things, and then you will be able to use both.' That started them trying for fun, and often the other children started to use their left hands, also for fun—excellent for both and no strain for either, as they didn't have to keep on long with their efforts."

How about those in the professions? There are many descriptions of jobs which are difficult for left-handers, but here is a good-luck story about a dentist, sent from Goring-on-Sea, Sussex—

"He is a sinistral but was made to write with his right hand in childhood. In his dental work he is completely ambidextrous which he finds a great help and he believes this is the result of being 'changed' as a child. He switches his instruments from hand to hand according to which part of the mouth he is working on and is thus able to keep standing on either side, moving behind the chair. He even pulls teeth with either hand which he tells me is not only more pleasant for the patient but much easier for the dentist, though he does not know any other dentist who is able to do this. I am sure his ambidexterity is a contributory factor . . . . His handwriting is bad —like a child's, and appears to be done with effort. He says he brushes his teeth with his left hand, which he regards as the sign of a true sinistral!"

A number of left-handed correspondents connect handedness with fortune-telling and the stars, though there is not much definite information available. The following is from Southampton—

"I was interested in the idea that a large proportion of left-handers are either, in the Zodiac, born under Gemini or Pisces. I am a left-handed Piscean myself. One of the characteristics of a Piscean is an 'artistic' bent. In view of the large numbers of left-handers who are authors, actors, painters, etc., it might be interesting to do a bit of research on the subject.

"My experience as a 'skiveller' seems to have been more fortunate than a number of people. My mother, a natural left-hander, was forced to use her right hand as a child, but became ambidextrous rather than neurotic. But she never made me do anything with my right hand, so I merely suffered the inconveniences attendant upon being a member of a minority group. Perhaps I am a representative of a (slightly) younger generation, and a more enlightened attitude. But oh, for watches that one can wind up without taking the thing off, and irons which wouldn't trip one up in a hideous snarl of flex!"

There have been, for years, letters about knitting and sewing. Here is a typical one from Dublin, Eire: "Although I am left-handed in some ways—dealing cards, opening screw-top bottles, etc.—I have failed miserably in teaching my daughter Elizabeth (a left-hander, age 6) to knit. Could some of your lady members give a few hints on left-handed knitting?"

This, from an eleven-year-old girl at Winchmore Hill, London, was prophetic in its anticipation of what has now become a reality.

"My mother is always complaining that this right-handed world is very difficult for left-handed people to live in. Scissors and tools and many knives are sharpened the wrong way for her. Kitchen utensils are often curved the wrong way. How about a shop where everything in it is for the use of left-handed people? I am sure it would be very well patronized."

In London, this is now possible, as in New York and in Paris. Other enlightened cities will surely follow, as the message gets through to the left-handers that the manufacturers are beginning to wake up to their needs.

On the purely practical side comes this rally-to-the-cause from an American living in Milan: "Good luck to the campaign, which I trust will include left-handed rifles, golf-clubs, motor-car mechanisms, light-switches, and enough space at dining-car tables and banquets to keep my left elbow and my right-handed neighbour's right elbow from slamming into each other at each bite."

Another protest comes from a woman in Stockton-on-Tees, Durham, about irons (fortunately her need is now catered for): "I approached Hoover some time ago regarding their damn silly flex on irons. I was told that they had to consider the right-handed majority of the population. Living in Yugoslavia, as I did, I found myself regarded as an oddity. The people were amazed to find that I was allowed to use my left hand for writing. In one Yugoslav village I literally stopped the band. I was scribbling my experiences in a note book, oblivious of the fact that the music had stopped, and some fifty men were gathered around the table, watching me. To this day I have never discovered whether they were amazed that I could write with such speed, or whether the use of my left hand intrigued them."

A correspondent from Harrow laments: "As a frustrated left-hander, that is, one who was made to do everything right-handed as a child, I am still, at nearly forty, suffering from the after-effects. I still use my left hand for all instinctive reactions, but I am now equally clumsy with both hands. My son aged 11 is left-handed, and as I watch him struggle with his handwriting, and see him blot his work as he goes over it with his right hand, I feel myself nearly thirty years back."

A letter from New South Wales: "I have heard left-handedness referred to here in Australia as 'Molly Dukes' [soft-handers]. I have also discovered that some schools over here still try and make left-handers change their writing to the right. Forty years ago in London

"Daddy-cat."
Drawn after the painting by Louis Wain in 1905.
Wain, left-handed, also ambidextral, was a famous
creator of animal pictures. His good cats were left-
pawed; his bad, right-pawed

some nitwits endeavoured to do the same to me, without success. So much so, that one teacher in later years referred to my scrawl as being that of an anaemic spider! I have always been drawn to the defence of minorities in every sphere—politics, sex, education, health, etc.—and now I wonder if it stems from my left-handedness. Why should minorities be forced to conform to 'get on' successfully? Who says that the majority is more 'natural' than the minority? There is a lot of philosophy in this left-handed business, in my opinion—I wonder if others agree?"

A schoolgirl from East Lothian writes: "In my year at school, there are six left-handers and all belong to the same group of friends, with the result that we have been called the Left-Handed League!"

Perhaps Left Power is coming, after all.

Left-handed People

A survey of famous Sinistrals and their champions through the centuries to the present day—Alexander the Great—Cicero and the Augurs—Charlemagne—King David and the Tribe of Benjamin— The Elizabethans—Dr. John Dee—Hans Holbein—Leonardo da Vinci—Sir Thomas Browne's Vulgar Errors—Benjamin Franklin— H. G. Wells—Ian Hay—General Tojo—Harpo Marx—A symposium of modern Sinistrals—A left-handed song by Michael Flanders

The young King Alexander the Great—it is remarkable to realize that he died in his thirty-second year—owed part of his education to Aristotle. His military exploits, particularly his conquest of Persia and the defeat of King Darius, are the main landmarks of his spectacular career. There is, however, the story recounted by several authorities, that at one stage of his campaign towards the east, he discovered a tribe which was completely left-handed (it could possibly have been the Dervishes, whose dances go widdershins) and which gave greater honour to the left hand as a form of greeting, because the left hand was considered to be nearer the heart.

There is a strange echo here with another warrior who turned philanthropist and educationalist, Lord Baden-Powell, founder of the Boy Scout Movement. Baden-Powell was himself ambidextral, and could even write simultaneously with both hands. As an officer in the Ashanti War of 1895, he once received the surrender of the chieftain of a town which had defended itself vigorously. As a token of respect Baden-Powell extended his right hand in greeting, but the chieftain explained that in his tribe the left hand was offered as a greeting for heroes.

Aristotle, Plato, Plutarch, Pythagoras—we know that all of them

78

Alexander the Great from a fresco in Pompeii

were interested in handedness or sidedness to a much greater extent
than most of their contemporaries. Theirs were years when superstition played a major part in the lives of men, but they also recognized
the practical implications of what was then not even described as a
"sinistral" state, with a derogatory meaning attached.

Perhaps Cicero (106–43 B.C.), senator, consul, governor and a
member of that select body, the Augurs, might originally have been
left-handed, for he suffered from a stammer—which did not,
apparently, impair his power of oratory in public. His forerunner
as a famous speaker, Demosthenes, also stammered, and in order to
alleviate his affliction practised speaking with pebbles in his mouth.
May not one assume, since the minority of left-handers is a
matter of genetics, and presumably has been a constant ratio through

the centuries, that both these two may have had their speech impaired through being "switched" forcibly in childhood?

"Man is a tool-using animal," wrote Thomas Carlyle (1795–1881) in *Sartor Resartus*. "Without tools he is nothing, with tools he is all." He realized that with the advent of tools in the Bronze Age, hand-preference developed, and added the theory that it may also have developed in primitive fighting. "Most important," he declared in his Journals, "to protect your heart and its adjacencies and to carry the shield on that hand." He added: "I wonder if there is any people barbarous enough not to have this distinction of hands: no human cosmos possible to have begun without it. . . . No organized manual labour could be carried on unless there were a common agreement as to which hand should be used for specialized tasks."

Hand preference, he concluded, is "a riddle, but it is the oldest human institution that exists." It may be asked why Carlyle, whose main preoccupation in literary life was first the French Revolution, then Frederick the Great, should have been interested in the subject. It was at the age of seventy-five that he lost the use of his right hand, and his restless mind turned to the cause and origins of handedness.

Charlemagne (A.D. 742–814), King of the Franks, Emperor of the West and conqueror of the Lombards and the Saxons, has often been credited with being left-handed, but no contemporary evidence can be quoted. As a patron of art and literature, under whom many classic masterpieces were preserved in monasteries, it may be that his artistic bent extended at least as far as ambidextrality.

King David came from the Tribe of Benjamin. The Hebrew words *ben yamin* mean "Son of the right hand." Yet it was known that there were many expert left-handed slingers among their warriors, and the most famous left-hander in Biblical history, Ehud the Benjamite, was chosen by the Lord to slay the King of Moab left-handedly, to take him by surprise. David was no ordinary, establishment monarch. A former shepherd boy, a musician, and a man credited with writing the Psalms (some of which are said to be authentic) he also in later life consorted with magicians and wizards, and conducted a celebrated séance with the Witch of Endor. Vague though the evidence may be, the implications are that David may well have been in the same category as the sinistral slingers of the tribe, which had always been the troublesome element among the children of Israel.

Between the time of the fall of Rome, the Byzantine period, the rise of Christianity in Europe, and the Renaissance, there is little evidence of any left-handed personality or movement. We have to turn to Britain in the sixteenth century for further reference.

The *scaevola*—Latin word for the left-hander—had always been an object of ridicule. The English Elizabethan dramatists all but ignored him—but surely there were enough fools and drolls and bumpkins among the creations of Shakespeare and his contemporaries to have had one or two of them dubbed as left-handed dolts. But, apart from a passing line or two from John Donne there is scarcely a reference. Donne's poem runs—

> *Reason is our Soule's left hand, Faith her right,*
> *By these we reach divinitie, that's you:*
> *Their loves, which have the blessings of your light,*
> *Grew from their reason, mine from fair faith grew.*

> *But as, although a squint left-handedness*
> *Be ungracious, yet we cannot want that hand.*
> *So would I, not to increase, but to expresse*
> *My faith, as I believe, so understand.*

Beaumont and Fletcher, Massinger ("a left-eyed knight is unlucky to meet"), Thomas Middleton ("I'll go and play left-handed Orlando among the madmen") and Ben Jonson have passing references, and that is all. It is a remarkable omission, in an age which explored every facet of human emotion, frailty and peculiarity. This, too, was an age in which superstition, augury ("We defy augury," said Hamlet: "there is a special providence in the fall of a sparrow"), good and bad luck, ghosts, witchcraft and wizardry were often mentioned, and indeed were sometimes made the central theme of the play.

Perhaps the most spectacular Elizabethan figure to have been, if not left-handed, at least ambidextrous, was Queen Elizabeth's Astrologer, Dr. John Dee, the "Magician of Mortlake," who almost deserves a chapter to himself for his influence at court, and his ritual routines, in which the magic rotation was undoubtedly "widdershins" (the way in which the witches in Macbeth go thrice round

Dr. John Lee, astrologer to Queen Elizabeth I

the cauldron in any enlightened production of the play) and the hand of power the left hand.

Dee was originally a mathematician. Elected a Fellow of Trinity College, Cambridge, he produced a play of Aristophanes there with such remarkable stage effects that he acquired the reputation, which he never lost, but later would have discarded, of being a magician. He then retired to Louvain University to study, but on returning to England he was charged by the Star Chamber with plotting against Queen Mary and practising sorcery. He was acquitted, and there were further journeys to Venice (1563) and, of all places, St. Helena. He later travelled to Hungary at the request of the Emperor Maximilian.

It was when he returned again to Mortlake that the Earl of Leicester and others invited him to choose a favourable date for the

6

coronation of Queen Elizabeth. It proved propitious, and he became a friend at court, often consulted in private conversation by the Queen, particularly at one time, when a passing comet had terrified the citizens of London. Elizabeth subsequently sent him as Ambassador to Poland, perhaps on secret service, and the Czar of Russia offered him the colossal retainer of £2,000 per year, which he refused, although it would have given him one of the highest places in Muscovy.

In his later years, after writing nearly fifty books on magic, he associated with the notorious magician Edward Kelly. Together they travelled throughout Europe, "raising spirits" in the traditional way, one describing the magic circle with the hazel wand, the other holding aloft a torch—both with the left hand. Later Dee gave up his partnership with Kelly, and was offered—so astonishing was his reputation—several offices of high position in the church. He became, eventually, a prosaic Warden of Manchester College, and endeavoured for the rest of his life to clear his name as a magician, and presumably a believer in the sinistral way of calling on the dead to rise.

So ended the remarkable career of the man who, among other things, invented the phrase "The British Empire"—strange claim for such a non-conforming personality.

One looks in vain in John Aubrey's *Brief Lives*, that unique, tabloid series of caustic character-sketches of uncertain veracity, tor any mention of a *scaevola*, although Aubrey, a distant cousin of Dr. Dee, whose short but eventful Life he includes, cheerfully describes Francis Bacon as a pederast.

John Milton made only two references to handedness: one in which Satan, in *Paradise Lost*, complains how hard it is for his legions to oppose "the red right hand of God," and the other curious reference in his *Reason of Church Government:* "This manner of writing . . . wherein, knowing myself to be inferior to myself, I have the use, as I may account it, but of my left hand." Hardly a right-handed compliment. The reference to the "red right hand" has a distinct analogy to the Red Hand of Ulster, where the wars were being fought in Milton's time.

Undoubtedly the most distinguished left-hander in England during Henry VIII's reign was the German artist Hans Holbein the

Younger. There is little direct reference to the sinistrality of the man who drew and painted the famous portraits of the King, Sir Thomas More, Lady Jane Seymour and other celebrities at court, but the pencil and brushwork are unmistakably made with the left hand, and there are certain left-handed characters in his series *The Dance of Death*.

The exact date of Leonardo's birth was not discovered until 1939, when Emil Moller pronounced it to be 15th April, in the year 1452. Details of Leonardo's life are well known, but some might be re-stated.

He was illegitimate, and born in Vinci: he was also found to be *scaevola*, or left-handed, and Vasari in his *Lives of the Painters*, describes how his grandfather grieved over this, since sinistrality was associated with the devil and all his works. But the works of Leonardo (unlike those, say, of Hieronymus Bosch and Goya, when drawing monsters) were anything but satanic. He was unmarried, and almost certainly homosexual.

His staggering output covered every field of human thought and activity. Like Michelangelo, he is thought to have been to some degree ambidextral but with a preponderant leaning to the left. Dimitri Merezhkovski, who wrote a novel on Leonardo's life, claims that he drew with the left hand and painted with the right. (The case of his most famous portrait of the Mona Lisa reveals that, in his preliminary drawings of her hands, the left hand is folded over the right: in the finished portrait the right hand is folded over the left— the instinctive position of a sinistral and a dextral respectively, so perhaps Leonardo the right-hander dictated the final position for painting.)

But for drawing and writing, Leonardo's contemporary colleague in science, Luca Paccioli, wrote *"scrivesi alla rovescia e mancina"* (*mancina* being the Italian for left-handed, as well as for untrustworthiness or evil). Paccioli also paid tribute to the "ineffable sweetness" of his drawing line. His scientific inventions were numerous and astonishing in their advance over the age in which he lived. The Space Age and Apollo capsules and landings on the moon would not have surprised the man who designed flying machines in the fifteenth century! As an anatomist he probably employed both hands (the ambidextral surgeon is always an asset to the profession,

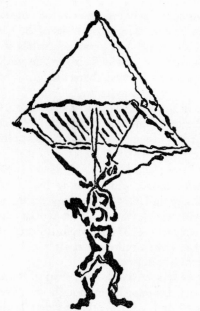

Leonardo da Vinci:
Sketch for man descending
with parachute

and Leonardo kept his anatomical table, full of specimens, next to his studio).

His writings, the famous, voluminous, Notebooks were all written left-handedly, in mirror-writing. There is no record of his having written with his right hand. In recent years, many more pages of his notebooks were discovered, the last seven hundred in Madrid in 1967. They have yet to be published: they are all in mirror-writing. It will never be known why he employed this style: the various theories include a theory among friends (though this could scarcely apply to about six thousand pages of serious material), his desire for secrecy, or a demonstration of heresy.

The learned doctor, theologian, and writer from Norwich, Sir Thomas Browne, is, even more than the divine Leonardo, the true hero of the sinistrals, though he may not be their patron saint, for he was dextral himself. He held that the right-handedness of the majority of human beings was a "sane and serviceable convention," but nothing more. In his vast work "*Vulgar Errors,*" an inquiry into "Very many Received Tenets and Commonly Presum'd Truths," he first took up the question of left-handed man in a right-handed world.

"It is most reasonable," he wrote, "for uniformity and sundry respective uses that man should apply himself to the constant use of one arm." But he added, "Dextral pre-eminence hath no regular or certain root in nature."

So the first blow was struck at the apparent Goliath-like status of the right-hander, and it was slung in favour of a left-handed David.

"Many, in their infancy, are sinistrously disposed," Browne continued, "and divers continue their lives left-handed . . . . I stand not yet assured which is the right side of man, or whether there be such a distinction in nature."

He added various references in history (including the story of the left-handed slingers of the tribe of Benjamin) and, as a practising doctor, dismissed the idea that handedness could come from a purely physical cause, such as the placing of the heart and liver. He decided that the true key to the matter was the brain, and its crossed laterality.

No man had, as far as is known, expressed this belief before, in medical terms.

Sir Thomas Browne's *Vulgar Errors* therefore contained, as early as 1648, good cheer for the left-handed minority, and more rational and medical explanation for their natural habits, than in all previous centuries, when sinistrality was so firmly linked, by Christian, Jew, Muslim, Hindu and Buddhist, with bad luck, the Devil, or anything clumsy or evil. But it was not until more than two hundred years later that the experts took up Browne's words, and started an additional examination into the causes of sinistrality. It was, in fact, the great neglected subject. To some extent, this is still the case.

The American genius Benjamin Franklin was not himself a left-hander but he wrote the following Letter from the Left Hand, as a "Petition to those in charge of Education," which brought the subject into the limelight once again.

"I address myself to all the friends of youth, and conjure them to direct their compassionate regard to my unhappy fate, in order to remove the prejudices of which I am the victim. There are twin sisters of us; the two eyes of man do not more resemble, nor are capable of being upon better terms with each other than my sister and myself, were it not for the partiality of our parents, who made the most injurious distinction between us. From my infancy I have been led to consider my sister as a being of a more elevated rank. I was suffered to grow up without the least instruction, while nothing was spared in her education. She had masters to teach her writing, drawing, music and other accomplishments; but if, by chance, I touched a pencil, a pen, or a needle, I was bitterly rebuked; and more than once I have been beaten for being awkward and wanting a graceful manner. It is true, my sister associated with me upon some occasions; but she always made a point of taking the lead, calling upon me only from necessity, or to figure by her side.

"But conceive not, sirs, that my complaints are instigated merely by vanity. No, my uneasiness is occasioned by an object much more serious. It is the practice of our family, that the whole business of providing for its subsistence falls upon my sister and myself. If any indisposition should attack my sister—and I mention it in confidence, upon this occasion that she is subject to the gout, the rheumatism, and cramp, without making mention of other accidents—what would be the fate of our poor family? Must not the regret of our parents be excessive, at having placed so great a difference between sisters who are so perfectly equal? Alas! We must perish from distress; for it would not be in my power even to scrawl a suppliant petition for relief, having been obliged to employ the hand of another in transcribing the request which I have now the honor to prefer to you.

"Condescend, sir, to make my parents sensible of the injustice of an exclusive tenderness, and of the necessity of distributing their care and affection among all their children equally.

"I am, with profound respect, Sirs,

Your obedient servant,
THE LEFT HAND"

Representatives of the neglected hand in the nineteenth century began to appear in greater numbers. Queen Victoria was ambidextral, as was her tutor in painting, Sir Edward Landseer. It was towards the end of the century that scientific and medical experts brought attention to the theories of handedness. In 1861, the English surgeon Robert Boyd declared that the left side of the brain was the heavier and more active. In 1883, the Italian Cesare Lombroso, who classed sinistrals with criminals, and was no friend of the left-hander, associated left-handedness with left-eyedness. The Scotsman Sir Daniel Wilson, who emigrated to Canada and became President of Toronto University in 1881, was himself a left-hander who pursued the subject in great detail. In 1902, at a Huxley Memorial Lecture, another Scotsman, Dr. D. J. Cunningham, declared that "right-handedness is due to a transmitted function of the left brain" and vice versa, a conclusion which Thomas Browne had reached in the seventeenth century. So we come to the twentieth century, and among men interested in the subject was H. G. Wells.

It would not be surprising if this author of so many science-fiction novels (the phrase was not known when he wrote books such as *The War of the Worlds, The First Men on the Moon*, and *The Shape of Things to Come*) had not considered the question of handedness. But he never made a detailed examination of the subject, and the only two relevant extracts from his work are part of a chapter from *Mr. Britling Sees it Through*, and *The Plattner Story*.

Mr. E. Connell of Halifax contributes this account from *Mr. Britling Sees it Through*. An American visitor had broken his right wrist, thanks to Mr. Britling's inexpert handling of his newly acquired motor car.

"It seemed as though Mr. Direck would be unable to write any letters until his wrist had mended. Teddy tried him with a type-writer, but Mr. Direck was very awkward with his left hand, and then Mr. Britling suddenly remembered a little peculiarity he had which it was possible that Mr. Direck might share unconsciously. Mr. Britling had found out quite by chance in his schooldays that while his right hand had been laboriously learning to write, his left hand, all unsuspected, had been picking up the same lesson, and that by taking a pencil in his left hand and writing from right to left, without watching what he was writing, and then examining the scrawl in the mirror, he could reproduce his own writing in exact reverse. About three people out of five have this often quite

unsuspected ability. He demonstrated his gift, and then Miss Cecily
Corner, who had dropped in in a casual sort of way to ask about
Mr. Direck tried it, and then Mr. Direck tried it. And they could
all do it. And then Teddy brought a sheet of copying carbon, and
so Mr. Direck, by using the carbon reversed under his paper, was
restored to the world of correspondence again."

As the correspondent points out, it is unlikely that three people
out of five have the ability to write in mirror-writing style, and that
in the years of the First World War, there would hardly be any over
the age of forty. Was H. G. Wells himself a shifted sinistral who was
unaware of it?

His story of Mr. Plattner the schoolmaster is even more odd.
Making a chemical experiment with a "greenish powder" found by
one of his pupils on the South Downs, Plattner was, according to the
tale, literally blown out of this world, into the fourth dimension of
space, and returned to earth, nine days later, left-handed. This, said
Wells, was the only way in which the left and right sides of a solid
body could be changed, and, apart from dwelling on the unfortunate
state of Plattner, the violently shifted dextral, he drew no moral,
which is a pity for those continually interested in the subject. It is
not known, for instance, what effect going into outer space, thoroughly protected and under instructions, has on the right-handed
astronaut seeking the moon (and most astronauts seem to be right-
handed). Certainly none of the Americans or Russians seem to have
suffered the fate of Wells's schoolmaster Gottfried Plattner.

Another alleged left-hander of the period is J. M. Barrie, creator
of *Peter Pan*. One looks in vain in the play for any mention of
handedness, though there was plenty of scope for it. The only footnote which can be added is the dilemma of a producer of the play,
which in his year ran twice daily, with a matinée and an evening
performance. The actors playing Captain Hook were a right-hander
during the early house, and a left-hander during the later show. The
whole duel routine between Hook and Peter had therefore to be
altered between performances—quite a problem for the actress
playing Peter!

There are few modern novels in which the hero is a left-hander.
One example, famous in its day, was *Pip: a Romance of Youth* by Ian
Hay (Major Ian Hay Beith), which first appeared in 1907.

The language has a sweet nostalgia. A girl is a "flapper," perhaps with a "retroussé nose and alluringly dimpled chin": unpleasant men are "utter outsiders" or even "d——d swine." A "pill" is not a contraceptive but a golf-ball. But in the end everything is "tophole" with "congratters" to the hero. Hay's style is "ripping."

The book is the story of a doctor's son (his sister was ironically called Pipette) who fell in love with a girl called Elsie, and played a game of golf with her, on the condition that if he won, she would agree to marry him.

Pip's sinistrality was discovered in early years, in the kitchen. "Emily, the kitchen-maid, made no objection to Pip stirring his tea with his knife; but what shocked her ideas of etiquette and deportment was the fact that he insisted on doing so with his left hand.

"Somehow, Pip's left hand was always getting into trouble. It was so officious; it was constantly usurping the duties and privileges of its fellow, such as cleaning his teeth, shaking hands and blowing his nose—literal acts of *gaucherie* that distressed Emily's gentle soul considerably."

But when the child became a schoolboy, and took up cricket, his sinistrality won him gradual fame. At nets, he bowled the Headmaster, an old Cambridge Blue, at the second delivery, and eventually went on to play for Cambridge himself. Perhaps the author was thinking of the great left-handed bowler of that day, Wilfred Rhodes, when he wrote the story.

In the famous golf match, in which he lost—and won—his "flapper" Elsie, no doubt Pip played right-handedly. Left-handed golf-clubs had not been introduced. But Ian Hay's hero is certainly a topping example of how a good sort can be left-handed.

As far as politics and statesmanship are concerned, the left-handers have little to quote on either side of the ledger. Perhaps the last left-handed Dictator was Julius Caesar (according to legend) or Alexander the Great, or Charlemagne. The Fascist and Nazi dictators—Franco, Hitler, Mussolini, and their henchmen—as well as the latter-day dictators such as Chairman Mao of China, Ho-Chi-Minh, President Tubman, General Ayub Khan, and the various Presidents of the Latin American Republics, all appear to be right-handed. America's last left-handed President was Harry S. Truman, and he signed documents with his right hand, while keeping his left for the bowling alley, and the President's throw at the start of the baseball season. Secretary Dean Rusk and Mr. Macnamara are also left-handed, so perhaps the U.S. will eventually have a substantial sinistral representation in the upper echelons of its political hierarchy. Britain's former Chancellor of the Exchequer, Mr. Roy Jenkins, is also left-handed—but then so, originally, was Mr. Harold Macmillan, former Conservative Premier. Converted in writing, he still shoots off the left shoulder in his favourite sport on the moors. In Africa, most rulers are known to be right-handed, but one of the sons of Chief Enahoro of Nigeria is left-handed, and allowed to continue to write as such.

Perhaps the most remarkable story of sinistrality among modern politicians comes from Japan.

General Hideki Tojo, ruler of Japan in the Second World War, was the only one of the enemy dictators to fall into Allied hands in 1945. Like Hitler, he attempted suicide, but the attempt failed—mainly because he was a left-hander (*hidarikiki* in Japanese).

The Tojo family, though not of the *Samurai* or higher caste, lived as retainers among feudal society. Courtney Browne, in his account of the General's life, *The Last Banzai*, describes him as "opinionated, obstinate, and quick to pick a fight" as a boy "and having got into a fight, he showed considerable personal courage in seeing it through." His school career was a poor one, for he was not only naturally left-handed (and since Japanese writing starts downwards, at the top right-hand corner, it is much easier for the right-hander) but also short-sighted, and his fellow schoolboys were amazed when he was accepted at a military preparatory school at the age of fifteen, and later at a military academy. He remained a soldier all his life. This is no place for the story of the man who was Prime Minister at the time of Pearl Harbour, who inflicted, in the earlier clashes with the Americans, the British, and Australians, those crippling blows which might have led to our defeat. But the tide of battle turned; the bombs were dropped on Hiroshima and Nagasaki in August, 1945, and in September, General MacArthur entered Tokyo. Tojo had already been deposed, and efforts were made to prevent him committing suicide, the traditional custom for a defeated Japanese soldier.

This he was determined to do, though not with the sword, in

the customary style of *hara-kiri*. Courtney Browne describes how his first act was to ask a neighbour, one Dr. Suzuki, to show him exactly where his heart was, and to persuade him to mark the spot with *sumi* ink used for brush-writing. Mrs. Tojo was outside the house dressed as a peasant, pretending to be weeding in the garden, when the Americans arrived to arrest her husband. She heard the shot, just before the G.I.s forced the door open.

Tojo only narrowly missed his heart, and the efforts to save his life—with a transfusion of American blood—eventually succeeded. But why had he failed? Mrs. Tojo later gave the probable explanation, when told that the bullet had entered the body at the wrong angle. Her husband was, she said, in many ways left-handed. "He would hold a hammer, tennis racket and other things with his left hand. I don't know which hand he held the pistol in but from his usual habit, I believe it was his left hand. Because he tried to hit his heart on the left side with his left hand, the bullet entered below and missed it."

One can see how awkward it must have been, to curve round the left arm to the left side (even though the heart is, if anything, almost central in the body). So Tojo lived long enough to be tried and executed, the first left-handed dictator since, perhaps, Alexander.

Alexander.
Coin of Lysimachus.

Harpo Marx, who died in 1964, leaving only Groucho alive among the trio, did not admit his left-handedness in his autobiography (as with so many sinistral life stories) but it is obvious from his films, and from the position of his harps. When he played with a symphony orchestra in Boston, the conductor was vaguely puzzled about him during rehearsals, and only after a long while did he realize what was peculiar: Harpo rested his instrument on the opposite shoulder. He seems to have been allowed, by his famous and indomitable mother, Minnie, to go on being left-handed, but then, as he admits, his career at New York City Public School 86 was scarcely a triumph. "At the age of eight, I was through with school and at liberty. Miss Flatto, my teacher, had said something had better be done to straighten me out, or I would be a disgrace to my family, my community and my country. The Harpo who went to college was a dog, a plum-coloured poodle. I never even finished the second grade."

This was certainly a case of a left-hander being the odd boy out—and continuing to act the part throughout his career.

In recent years, recognition of left-handedness has revealed many notable people: in the higher echelons of society and politics, they range from President Saragat of Italy, a *mancino* (and the Italian word has a doubtful meaning), who has paid the author the compliment of congratulating him on his investigations, to the Crown Prince of Iran, son of the Shah, heir to the Peacock Throne. Prince Reza Shah, a young boy, has a mother, in Queen Fara Diba, who was educated at the Sorbonne and is thoroughly modern-minded in a traditional Muslim country. It is always surprising to find that a Muslim is permitted to be left-handed, but for a Crown Prince it is unique. Other left-handed Muslims include the former Jordanian Ambassador to Britain, Mr. Mehta, and the Director of Culture in Libya.

In political circles, at Westminster, we can also repeat the names of British politicians like the late Aneurin Bevan who had a stammer (being a switched sinistral, which became deadly in parliamentary debate), Mr. Roy Jenkins, Mr. J. P. W. Mallalieu, Mr. Gerald Kaufman, and many a rank-and-file Member of Parliament.

Mr. Huntington Hartford, the multi-millionaire chain-store head, also puts down his stammer to the fact that he was forced to use his

right hand. There have been many sinistral American film-stars—
Judy Garland, Betty Grable, Kim Novak, Olivia de Havilland
among the ladies, and Rod Steiger and Rock Hudson among the
men. Cole Porter composed music from his invalid-chair left-
handedly. Milton Caniff, a noted lawyer, carries his brief in his left
hand.

In Britain, the same is true. In proportion to the average of left
and right as a whole, the celebrities seem much more numerous.
To those who like left-handed name-dropping, one can enumerate
the following: Sir Compton Mackenzie, Mervyn Stockwood,
Bishop of Southwark, Godfrey Winn the writer, and the 17th
Viscount Falkland. Among artists and cartoonists, Ronald Searle,
creator of the sinistral and therefore devilish St. Trinian's girls, who
paraded the mini-skirt long before it became the vogue in 1968;
Brockbank of *Punch*; William Rushton of *Private Eye*; Mervyn Levy
the art critic.

Among what are called, in the brochures, Stars of Stage and
Screen can be named people like Rex Harrison, who made all
Professor Higgins's notes in *My Fair Lady* with his left hand; two of
the Beatles, Paul McCartney and Ringo Starr; the singer who was
Paul McCartney's protégée, Mary Hopkin; Jessie Matthews, the
once-famous Mrs. Dale of radio; Kenneth Williams, who is also an
expert left-handed calligraphist; Jean Shrimpton, Terence Stamp,
Jeremy Brett, Marianne Faithfull, Eric Porter, Leslie Crowther,
Richard Wattis, all following in the lead set by Harpo Marx and
that greatest left-handed all-rounder in history, Charlie Chaplin.

In these days of intricate machinery, the left-hander is obviously
at a disadvantage. There is nothing more right-handed than an IBM
computer! So it was with great joy, I hope, that sinistrals all over the
world learned that one of the latest team of Astronauts was left-
handed. The *New York Herald-Tribune* in Paris broke the news. The
first-ever sinistral Moon Man was Commander Gordon. But even
so, he was the odd Moon-man out, for his was the thankless task of
orbiting the moon in loneliness, while his two colleagues clumped
around with those enormous rucksacks, picking up pebbles and dust.
Did Commander Gordon recall, as he continued circling, that the
Moon herself, the "Earth's pale consort," is associated with the left
hand and the distaff side?

"Katina," Miss Katina Theodossiu, is a well known astrologer, whose numerous activities range from the popular, bulk-prediction of the stars for readers of a London evening newspaper, to individual horoscopes made for private individuals (tycoons and politicians among them). She has also master-minded an American venture of horoscopes by computer, which looks like making big business.

Katina was an only child, and the only left-hander in the family. "I was not switched over, but for a time I was blind in my left eye, and it may be that, as normal writing went from left to right, and I had to look leftward with my right eye, I found it easier to use the left hand to hold the pen. I think there are a number of people who come to left-handedness through some slight physical handicap.

"But I don't think that in my professional life I've found anyone who has actually suffered from being left-handed, or has had any inferiority complex—any chip on the left shoulder, as it were. In fact, most of my fellow sinistrals think of themselves as rather a distinguished lot. If left-handedness is a hereditary factor, then it may indeed make left-handers more individualistic and conscious of themselves. If, alternatively, there's no hereditary factor, then it may be accounted for, as perhaps in my case, by a physical handicap."

On the subject of superstition against the left hand she agreed that it went far back into mythology, and cited the case of Uranus being castrated sinistrally. "All these dark superstitions arise from the old astronomical ideas which lie at the bottom of all religions, and that's the origin of it. In the old days, if you were in a minority—the odd man out—somebody wanted to chuck a stone at you. But there's no such prejudice today."

Left-handers are mainly individualists, says Miss Theodossiu. No wonder then that a high proportion of actors—and in particular, comedians—are sinistral, usually with more than a touch of satire, such as Rex Harrison, Kenneth Williams, Harpo Marx, Charlie Chaplin, Michael Flanders, and Richard Wattis, who portrays imperturbable and impenetrable civil servants.

"I'm not totally left," he admits. "I kick with the left foot, but in tennis, cricket and golf—when I get the time for them—I use the right hand."

At school they said "Knock it out of him!" but Mr. Wattis was another of those whose perceptive parents stood by his instinct, again because of the theory that a change might cause a stutter. There is no known history of left-handedness in the family.

"I'm conscious that other left-handed people look awkward, particularly in writing. I can in fact write with both hands, but my right-handed style has no character at all, whereas, to make a boast, I think my left-handed writing is rather nice. It was certainly consciously acquired at school, sometimes through copying somebody else. People have told me, 'I wouldn't have thought you were left-handed because you write so well.' That's possibly because my writing doesn't slope backwards, as so much left-handed writing does. It's part of me, and I certainly tried to write well when I was young.

"I'm the most ghastly person in a car," adds Wattis. "The moment I want the driver to turn left, I say, 'No, turn *right* here' and vice versa, so they never know where they are!"

Dr. Macdonald Critchley cites the example of a dyslexic taxi-driver in Copenhagen, who had so little sense either of going left or right that he used to put a black mark on the right thumb nail when directed to a particular suburb. To anticipate such a contingency, he always kept a piece of black chalk in his pocket.

But no one would accuse Mr. Wattis of being dyslexic.

Another left-hander proud of his handwriting style is comedian Kenneth Williams, who lists as his hobby in *Who's Who:* "calligraphy," a rare claim for a sinistral.

A magazine editor, Paul Johnson formerly of the *New Statesman,* declares he had no chip at all on his shoulder. "There was never any question of changing me over—indeed, my parents were very anxious not to interfere with my natural instinct"—and he goes on to refer to the possibility of impediment in speech as a result, and referred to the well-known example of King George VI.

"I didn't develop any sense of guilt, either, as some left-handers do. I was lucky with my teachers: none of them tried to force me to conform to the right-handed writing." (Mr. Johnson writes in the "hook" style, very quickly and fluently.)

"It may be," he goes on, "that the left-hander suffers because right-handedness is written into our moral thinking, as it were. But there's another aspect. I'm a left-winger as well as a left-hander, and

"And now you shall listen to
the Left-hand *side of the story . . ."*

I associate 'right' with evil and 'left' with good, so this possibly explains why I don't feel ashamed of being left-handed. To me 'right' means the Establishment, Fascism, extreme conservatism, and the kind of people who believe in flogging and hanging and that sort of thing, whereas the 'left' I associate with enlightenment, a rational approach to politics, the process of thinking with your brains rather than thinking with your bowels: all these desirable qualities I associate with the left."

From a radio interviewer and reporter, Tim Matthews, comes this comment—

"I'm one of a family of seven and no one else in the family is in any way left-handed. I seem to have come out of the blue. No one tried to change me, otherwise, it appears, I might have stuttered, and that wouldn't have done in my profession! I'm left-footed, too. And left-eyed. This did me no good when I went into the Army. I found sloping arms very difficult, and they used to put me in the back row of the back platoon of the back company as I was obviously a disgrace to the Army."

(There is, in fact, a phrase "the left-handed soldier of the line," which means the man who is the last man at the very left, who therefore cannot collide with his neighbour should he make any sinistral gesture.)

"I found, too, that guns were the wrong way round. So being a hopeless soldier I took the first opportunity of getting into radio, partly to avoid using right-handed equipment for killing people.

"One other thing I can't stand is seeing other left-handed people writing. It makes me feel all funny inside. My eating habits are fairly right-handed, but I'm fascinated by the American way of eating, cutting up the meat first, switching the knife over to the left, and using the right fork, a double switching. It rather intrigues me, which is more than I can say for the type of American food I've been eating."

Many left-handers share this dislike of seeing fellow-sinistrals write, or of meeting them in sport (as with Gary Sobers, for instance, and Rod Laver, the left-handed world champion tennis player).

This is not always the case, in the opinion of journalist James Green of the London *Evening News*.

"I don't think a left-hander notices another left-hander," he says. "There were none in my family and both my children are right-handed." But obviously Mr. Green's first teacher noticed it: "When I was about seven, the master did attempt to make me write right-handedly, but my father heard of this and said if it happened he'd take me away. My problem, of course, was writing—the master could see that. With the old-fashioned pen you're pushing it towards your body, so you can easily mark or blot the paper, and then get a clump round the ear for dirty work.

"I also had the old cack-handed problem over rifles during the war, but even when I joined the Navy—Fleet Air Arm—I was 'dipped' on my first test. In fact, nine of us failed altogether, and when we lined up and compared notes, we found we were *all* of us left-handed!

"In my opinion, the right-hander assumes, because he's in the majority, that it's the left-hander who's always out of step: that it's rather like having a slice at golf—it's something you should get over, get rid of. In golf, by the way, the left-hander seems more likely to slice to the left, in my experience, and if he does, he may find the ball's in the rough, and his feet are on the fairway. You can't win, in that case."

Dr. Robin Wilson, elder son of Mr. Harold Wilson, says—

"As a teacher, being left-handed helps a lot. Right-handed teachers often walk in front of what they have just written on the blackboard, whereas we don't have to worry about this. I am all in favour of not 'changing over' in schools. Luckily my parents were very sensible about this. Both my cousins on my mother's side are left-handed. I am not sure whether I'm in favour of too many left-handed gadgets just for the sake of having them. For instance, right-handed notebooks can be used from the back end by those who want to, and the prospect of left-handed cheque books doesn't excite me. Corkscrews and scissors are what I need most.

"I didn't like the way some left-handed children in the U.S. are taught to write 'upside down' (the hook style) so that they can see what they are writing. This seems to me to be unnecessary, and the results are usually unreadable . . . . However, left-handed people are said to be better at reading upside down—not very important but interesting."

Michael Flanders, internationally known as a poet and entertainer, particularly with his partner Donald Swann, has lost the use of his nether limbs, but not his sense of humour. From his wheel-chair have come many witticisms which have delighted London and New York. In a note specially intended for this book he declares—

"I am totally left-handed in all my gestures and mannerisms. I still have to remember to shake hands with my right hand and, during the war, fought a constant (losing) battle against my instinct to give a left-handed salute.

But I wonder if today my uninhibited left-handedness isn't a help to me in my profession? In my usual role as entertainer describing shared experience directly to an audience, or as presenter standing between them and the action, do they perhaps find it easier to recognize in me a mirror image of themselves, 'held up to nature,' as t'were?

Like all the most fascinating theories this can't be proved. But I do seem to notice an unusual number of left-handers among actors. As the odd men out of the world's oldest minority—cack-handed with most tools and weapons—have we always gravitated to the roles of clowns, fools and jesters?"

Mr. Flanders added that his daughter Laura is left-handed, "though, like most of us, she has acquired a degree of dexterity in a right-handed world. We suspect that her six-month-old sister, Stephanie, is the same."

As an example of the humour he can extract from a true situation in the world, he evolved a song about the right-handed honeysuckle and the left-handed bindweed, whose habits he had observed in an exhibition of plants at the Natural History Museum in London.

MISALLIANCE

The fragrant Honeysuckle spirals clockwise to the sun
And many other creepers do the same.
But some climb counterclockwise, the Bindweed does, for one,
Or Convolvulus, to give her proper name.

Rooted on either side a door, one of each species grew,
And raced towards the window-ledge above.
Each corkscrew to the lintel in the only way it knew,
Where they stopped, touched tendrils, smiled, and fell in love.

Said the right-handed Honeysuckle
To the left-handed Bindweed:
"Oh let us get married
If our parents don't mind, we'd
Be loving and inseparable,
Inextricably entwined, we'd
Live happily ever after,"
Said the Honeysuckle to the Bindweed.

To the Honeysuckle's parents it came as a shock.
"The Bindweeds," they cried, "are inferior stock.
They're uncultivated, of breeding bereft.
We twine to the right, and they twine to the left!"

    Said the counterclockwise Bindweed
    To the clockwise Honeysuckle:
    "We'd better start saving,
    Many a mickle makes a muckle,
    Then run away for a honeymoon
    And hope that our luck'll
    Take a turn for the better,"
    Said the Bindweed to the Honeysuckle.

A bee who was passing remarked to them then:
"I've said it before, and I'll say it again,
Consider your offshoots, if offshoots there be.
They'll never receive any blessing from me.

"Poor little sucker, how will it learn
When it is climbing, which way to turn.
Right—left—what a disgrace!
Or it may go straight up and fall flat on its face!"

    Said the right-hand thread Honeysuckle
    To the left-hand thread Bindweed:
    "It seems that against us all fate has combined.
    Oh my darling, oh my darling,
    Oh my darling Columbine,
    Thou art lost and gone for ever,
    We shall never intertwine."

Together they found them the very next day.
They had pulled up their roots and just shrivelled away,
Deprived of that freedom for which we must fight,
To veer to the left or to veer to the right!

The Devil's Dictionary from A to Z

If the Devil is presumed, as superstition would have it, to be left-handed, and left-handedness is associated with clumsiness, uncleanness and non-conformity, in addition, then it is necessary to provide sinistrals with an appropriate guide or *vade-mecum* to take with them in a right-handed world.

The larger issues of handedness—handwriting, speech defects, religious practices, educational tests and case-histories—have been treated in separate chapters.

Here are some of the additional factors, ranging from Ambidexterity to Zangwill. Here, indeed, is much challenging information, arranged alphabetically. Here is much of the ammunition necessary for a self-respecting sinistral—and to the devil with dextrals!

AMBIDEXTERITY

It was Adolphe-Jean Focillon, nineteenth-century French scientific writer, who declared—

"The hands are not a pair of passively identical twins. Nor are they to be distinguished like two children of unequal value; one trained in all skills, the other a serf. I do not believe in the eminent dignity of the right hand. Deprived of the left, it retires into a painful, almost sterile solitude."

An argument might be made out that as humans we should follow the precepts of our ancestors, the apes, and be ambidextrous. Many skilled men have been—Leonardo da Vinci for one. Most left-handers have to acquire, owing to social or mechanical pressures, some degree of ambidextrality. Sportsmen are often adept at the use of either hand, particularly in baseball, cricket, and lawn tennis. It is when a writer like Focillon uses the word "dignity" that something more than the mere manual skill creeps in. Once give the preferred hand a status, and surround it with all the glamour of righteousness and power, and you have made hand-dominance into a religious as well as a practical thing. Here the mystique and the mischief lies.

It is agreed by most experts that, within the first year, children use either hand indiscriminately. Preference can be induced or, if the child is left free, can be inferred, and encouraged on its own course. "An ambidextrous child," writes Dr. Margaret Clark, "or, to be more exact, one who has no preference for either hand, will quickly appear to be right-handed" (for reasons of imitation, training, and the right-handed nature of everyday objects). "This group consists of those who are equally good with both hands, and would for that reason have been able easily to adjust themselves to left-handedness had society so required." Children skilful with either hand, she adds, often acquire this special, double facility, of being good with the right hand, coupled with an ability to make use of the left when occasion demands it.

It is agreed also, in some professions such as the medical, that adaptability for either hand is an advantage, particularly when an ambidextral surgeon has an arduous operation to perform, in which the scalpel or similar instrument can be passed from one hand to the other.

The ambidextral ability can, of course, be developed indefinitely —it can be of great help in conjuring and sleight-of-hand as well as in sport and surgery. But all this may be seen as a *tour-de-force* rather than as an innate habit. Historians of handedness, however, rarely omit to mention the efforts of one John Jackson, who in 1905 founded the Society for Ambidextral Culture and Upright Writing, declaring "There is no disadvantage, but every advantage, in our being truly ambidextrous. Why cannot man be ambidextrous again?"

Dr. Clark notes that as a result of Jackson's work "many infant schools introduced two-handed training, and copy-books were even prepared for this. Its main interest now is that it accounts for the

view held so often by people of a certain age-group that ambidexterity is the ideal."

Jackson had many powerful supporters, the most famous being
the man who signed the introduction to his book with both hands,
simultaneously, Major-General Baden-Powell, hero of the Ashanti
War and later to become founder and Chief of the Boy Scout movement. Is this the origin of the left-handed handshake, symbol of the
Boy Scouts? Indeed it is. Baden-Powell, in his military campaign in
Africa, had found a tribe which honoured their Great Ones by
offering the left hand in greeting. In the spirit of Lawrence of
Arabia, Baden-Powell accepted the greeting, and made it his own,
almost masonic, mark for his young followers. Other supporters
included the eminent Canadian, Sir Daniel Wilson, who worked
with a pen in the right hand and a pencil in the left, the painter Sir
Edwin Landseer, also ambidextral and capable of drawing two
pictures simultaneously (he was also art instructor to the ambidextral Queen Victoria) and a distinguished Committee of
fifty.

But Jackson did not live to see his Ambidextral Society "for the
promotion of Educational Reform and Two-handed Training"
come to fruition. At least it made a stir, and left-handed man, who is
usually at an advantage when it comes to the use of his other hand,
may regret its passing. At least something of its ideal exists in the new
ambidextral instruments and gadgets now available in everyday
life.

*"We've got a split
personality, you and I"*

APHASIA (LOSS OF SPEECH)

C. S. Orton, the American expert on speech and handwriting problems, makes these two definitions—

"*Aphasia:* acquired. A loss in the power of expression of speech, due to injury or disease of the brain centres." "*Aphasia:* developmental. A failure in development of speech or speech understanding which is not the result of deafness in the peripheral speech mechanism."

This impediment, which has for many years baffled mankind in accounting for those, not born without speech, but "struck dumb," has been the subject of intense study over the last century. Speech is, of course, not the privilege of mankind, highest of the animal species. Other animals can communicate with each other in ways far more subtle than *homo sapiens*, who can devise a television commercial but has not perfected a mating call.

Lord Brain finds the first reference to man's speech in the Book of Genesis—

"And out of the ground the Lord God formed every beast of the field, and every fowl of the air; and brought them unto Adam, *to see what he would call them* . . . ."

In so far as the study of handedness is concerned, it is necessary to discover the connexion between speech and preferred laterality, a connexion close and critical. To quote Dr. Abram Blau: "scientific observations, especially from case studies in clinical neurology and psychiatry, later in psychology and education, have proved this tie-up beyond a shadow of doubt. The first hint of this association came to light nearly a century ago when aphasia was discovered. It became apparent that certain injuries to the brain led to loss of language capacity and much of our knowledge of the cerebral physiology of language was derived from these symptoms. In such cases of brain injury the extent and character of speech disturbances, or reading or writing disabilities were studied . . . ."

Blau, however, did not believe that handedness is a heredity trait, and his subsequent investigations have been challenged, though this is a good first definition.

We know that, when a person has a stroke, one side of his body becomes affected, and often useless. It is widely held that the *opposite* hemisphere of the brain, in which the stroke occurred, has been the cause. But the stroke has to come first, before it can be established whether the patient is right- or left-handed. One can, in other words, but wait and see, because man is a "humanitarian" human. Experiments in animals can lead us so far and no further, although when rats were used in a test-case, an operation in one side of the brain altered the use of the paw on the opposite side.

Aphasia is an important medical subject in itself today, and many of the experiments have offered evidence on handedness. "A century ago," declares Professor Oliver Zangwill of Cambridge, "Dr. Hughlings Jackson put forward his notion of the leading hemisphere —the precursor of our modern concept of cerebral dominance."

"The two brains," wrote Jackson, "cannot be mere duplicates if damage to one alone can make a man speechless. For those processes, there must be one side which is leading . . . ." It was Zangwill who challenged the accepted idea of crossed laterality, and held that the left side of the brain might well be the dominant side in the majority of left-handers as well as right-handers.

Zangwill comments "recovery from aphasia is more complete in patients who are left-handed or who have left-handed parents than in those who are fully right-handed." This is apparently because left cerebral laterality is more prevalent than right.

An interesting historical footnote is provided by Dr. Macdonald Critchley, who has made a study of the illnesses of several distinguished historical characters, including Oscar Wilde, Napoleon III, and Dr. Samuel Johnson, who suffered a stroke in 1783, and found his speech had gone. Since the great Doctor noted everything about himself, he wrote, on the first day of his infirmity on 17th June: "It hath pleased almighty God this morning to deprive me of the powers of speech." He added "I think my case is not past remedy. By a speedy application of stimulants much may be done. I question if a vomit vigorous and rough would not rouse the organs of speech to action." Johnson recovered within a week, and Critchley adds this important observation—

"Another possible explanation of the transient and mild character of Dr. Johnson's aphasia comes up for discussion. We have to consider the possibility that Dr. Johnson might have been left-handed, and that no frank unilateral cerebral dominance existed. We believe that in left-handers, cerebral lesions, whether of the right or left hemispheres, are apt to be followed by a speech impairment of the benign type. From a study of Dr. Johnson's upbringing it is not possible to state with confidence whether he was left-handed or right-handed. We know from Johnson's own diary that an 'issue' was cut in his left arm which was deliberately kept open and was not allowed to heal until he was six years old. Probably this was a device to cure his defective eyesight.

"It is indubitable that the Doctor habitually wrote with his right hand, but this must not be taken as an argument for right manual preference . . . . There is but one picture which would appear to argue in favour of a left-sided preference. In the well-known illustration of Johnson entertaining two pretty Methodists, a teacup lies on the table on the left side.

"But no single test of handedness has been so far discovered by medical men."

Dr. Heberden, a famous surgeon in his day, was chiefly responsible for the treatment of Johnson. He wrote in his *Commentaries:* "When a person has been struck on the left side, and has at the same time lost his voice, there is no certainty of his being able to signify his feelings, or his wants, by writing . . . ."

Johnson in fact partially recovered from his stroke, and lived on for another eighteen months.

There is one more scrap of evidence provided by Boswell, when he and Johnson were dining with the King of France, Louis XVI.

"We observed that His Majesty ate with his left hand: and so did we."

Whether this was out of loyalty to a sinistral Monarch, or whether it suggests that both Boswell *and* Johnson were dominantly left-handed, we shall never know. If so, it would be a magnificent partnership to add to the long roll of left-handed celebrities.

Critchley ends his essay with an observation which, if it has nothing to do with aphasia or handedness, is perhaps the most pleasant of all the great Doctor's many observations—

"If I had no duties, and no reference to futurity, I would spend my life driving briskly in a post-chaise with a pretty woman; but she should be one who could understand me, and would add something to the conversation . . . ."

If she got a word in, edgeways.

BABY, HOLDING THE

On which arm does a mother rest her baby? Statistics on this have been conflicting since the days of Plato, who first attributed the weakness of the left side to the bad habits established by nurses and mothers. If a right-handed mother carried her offspring on her left arm, to leave her right hand free, then the child's left arm would be free, too, and might develop more quickly and become the preferred hand. If this were proven, it would obviously mean that right-handed mothers would have left-handed children, which is absurd. It is obviously much more the deliberate act of handing objects to an infant, and observing which hand he instinctively uses to clutch them, which determines (and can alter) his handedness.

There is no exhaustive research on handedness in mothers, but clearly the Platonic theory is, in this case, wrong.

The enterprising Cyril Burt added a footnote (or should it be handnote?). He considered the most famous mother-and-child portraiture in history. Here are his results: "I have examined a hundred well-known pictures of the Madonna and Child, and find that fifty-nine have the child on the left, and only forty-one on the right: with the earlier painters, in particular, the left position seems commoner."

The proportion, however, seems surprisingly even. Could it be assumed that, since quite a number of painters were, if not left-handed, at least ambidextral, like Michelangelo, that it was the painter who decided the position of mother and child, rather than the woman who sat for the painting, with or without a real baby in her arms? Raphael is a case in point (he also has been credited with ambidextrality). Burt compares two great paintings: the Sistine Madonna and the Madonna del Granduca. In the one, the child is on the mother's right: in the other, on her left. Yet in both, the left hand is beneath the child, to bear its weight, and the right hand is free.

BICYCLES

Cyril Burt has the following comment to make: "When as a child I first learned to cycle, I mounted and dismounted, like most people, from the left-hand side of the machine. Later it seemed desirous to practise doing so from the opposite side. I practised assiduously; and then found to my astonishment that, in cultivating the new habit, I had also formed a new impulse. It proved singularly difficult, and indeed, almost annoying, to go back to what had been the more natural mode."

All mounting steps still existing on the sides of roads are on the left side of the road: this is a strong argument that, originally, travellers kept to that side.

A correspondent in Torquay, Devon comments: "With reference to the driving of vehicles in this country on the left-hand side of the road: as a cyclist and not a car driver, I could not mount on the left-hand side, so that while putting my right foot on the right pedal I was exposed to the dangers of the middle of the road, so that I would welcome driving on the right."

BIRDS

Whether Shakespeare knew all about the rules of augury, we cannot say, though his knowledge of classical superstition makes it very likely. Hamlet knew that there was a special providence in the fall of a sparrow. The flight of birds has been, from the days of Romulus and Remus, and the founding of Rome, a matter of great significance in so far as right and left are concerned.

Bird life today, however, has not much to offer for the student of left-handedness, although the naturalist and painter Peter Scott, himself left-handed and a specialist in depicting birds in flight, is not always sure in which direction they should be flying.

Parrots, according to observation, in Zoos, usually perch on the right foot, or claw, and feed themselves with the left claw. This does not necessarily determine which is the dominant claw.

Magpies, cuckoos, robins and ravens were all at one time considered birds of good or ill omen. A Devon man is, according to the old superstition, to spit over his right shoulder three times if he sees a magpie.

The *corva sinistra*—the crow or raven on the left—is a particularly bad omen. Ravens, anyhow, were precursors of death, as Lady Macbeth well knew when a raven croaked as Duncan entered her castle.

One would not expect the little wren to be implicated in the matter, but the following interesting note comes from the Nature Notes by Maurice Burton in the London *Daily Telegraph* in March, 1969—

"When I wrote here several weeks ago about wrens catching small fishes I did so with some trepidation. Although there are records of this in the reputable literature on birds, they are few, so that I felt I was on slightly uncertain ground. I need not have worried. A number of readers have favoured me with their own accounts of having seen this."

In one of the more detailed of these the writer describes living on a farm in the north-east of Scotland in his youth and often seeing wrens on the riverside catch small trout, up to an inch or so long, but never minnows or sticklebacks.

A further point of interest in this letter is that the wrens, after catching a fish, "bashed it on a stone and stunned it, then placed their right foot, always the right one, on the head and pecked at the tail end and tore off a long strip up towards the head.

"We are accustomed to the idea of right- and left-handedness in people. There have been many studies of this in monkeys also. Those who are experienced with horses find that they are left-handed or right-handed. And why not? We do not have the monopoly of physical attributes, so we ought to expect this in all animals in some form or another.

"Birds have lost their hands but they could be left- or right-footed."

BLACK MASS

This ceremony still survives, apparently, today. In the present per-missive society, witchcraft continues, and modern witches give interviews on television and are featured in colour-supplements. Black Mass is a deliberate, anti-Christian ceremony, with everything performed the other way round, that is, left-handedly and widder-shins. But the Black Mass of today is a pale, shrinking shadow of what it was, we are led to believe, in medieval times, and in eighteenth-century France, when Madame de Montespan was very willing, though scarcely eligible, to play the essential part of the naked virgin on the altar, ready to be christened with the blood of a slaughtered child poured into a chalice placed between her breasts, by a bogus priest who was then designated to copulate with her, as part of the proceedings.

The love and legend of the Black Mass is so divergent and confused—it ranges from books and "X" certificate films like *Rosemary's Baby* to learned treatises—that the actual ritual of it is difficult to define. The naked virgin on the altar was a useful peg on which to hang what turned out to be in most cases a very humdrum affair. But the essential fact about the Black Mass is that it was anti-Christian—in other words, it was anti-right-handed, since all the Christian symbols were reversed, the Lord's Prayer was read backwards, the Devil (as a goat) was God, and every action taken was in violation of the Christian way of life. Devil-worship was goat-religion, ending, in the Witches' Covens, with the kissing of the goat's hindquarters—the origin of that popular phrase, "kiss my arse." This was, in fact, the last act which had to be performed after His Satanic Majesty had appeared before the Witches' Coven in the shape of a goat. This kissing of the Devil occurs many times in the testimonies of alleged witches confessing at their trials.

Today we can dismiss all this mumbo-jumbo as the psychological aberrations of a minority of mentally-handicapped people—and this is probably what it was. One has only to read Aldous Huxley's description of the Devils of Loudun in France, or the record of the Witches of Salem, in America, to realize that this kind of madness could involve whole communities, who would otherwise have been living normal lives.

The Black Mass can be as lurid or as dreary as you wish, according to the ritual specified. In his *Treasury of Witchcraft*, Harry E. Wedock, an American author, declares, dramatically—

"One of the most tenebrous and malefic performances among witchcraft practices, the Black Mass, grew in geographical extent and in rampant prevalence, reached its demoniac apogee in the Middle Ages, continued potently though secretly into the Middle Ages, and made its deepest impression in French Society." Hence Madame de Montespan.

CIGARS, CIGARETTES
"Have a good cigar." That is an invitation to accept a cigar in which

Sacrificing a child to the Devil at a Witches' Coven

the leaf has been rolled by hand. The veining on the dried tobacco leaf turns almost invariably in the same direction, and the skilled cigar-roller is almost invariably right-handed. But it is a known fact that—as with the famous sinistral whelk—very occasionally a left-handed leaf turns up, which has to be rolled the other way. Exact ratios are difficult to ascertain, but the possibility is always there. Vegetation is not entirely symmetrical or dextral.

Martin Gardner adds this about cigarettes—"Cigarettes contain levinicotine, an asymmetric carbon compound in the alkaloid family. (In this sense we can say that our cylindrical cigarettes are all left-handed!) Levinicotine is found in all tobacco plants. But there is a right-handed form of nicotine, dextronicotine, which is *never* found in tobacco plants."

So left-handers can go on happily smoking sinistral cigarettes even under the threat of lung cancer, if they only mildly inhale what left-handed Sir James Barrie called *My Lady Nicotine*.

CIRCUMAMBULATION

When you enter a shop or public building which you do not know, do you turn instinctively to the left or right, or keep straight on? Much will depend, of course, on what you are seeking, and what your eye catches. If it is a museum with an inquiry or admission desk on one side or the other, you will immediately turn to that side. But an inquiry held by an American department store revealed a predominant number turning instinctively to the right—therefore the management arranged whatever tempting bargain display they had to be put up on that side. The author's own instinctive movement is to turn to the left, and his own modest inquiries have revealed that this is a sinistral tendency. Therefore, the theory that the movement of the earth to the right is responsible cannot be valid. It is far more likely that one's instinctive hand-movements are the cause. It could also be part of the ancient and once immensely important practice of circumambulation, which has permeated all forms of ritual, religion and superstition throughout the world, and still survives in many forms.

Christianity soon took up the ritual movement from left to right, clockwise. It is said that, when St. Patrick consecrated Armagh, he led the procession of the faithful in this fashion, and thus gave the official blessing to the movement. In time, to go round a church anti-clockwise was deemed to be blasphemy or witchcraft, and could be punishable by hanging.

It is of interest to note that the Gaelic language contained many variations on the word *widdershins*, among them *widdenshynnes*, *widderson*, *witherways*, *witherwardis*, *wodderwardis*, *witherwise*. It was derived originally from the old German word *widersin*, "against the direction."

The ancient Gaelic word for the actual movement was *deisol* or *deisel*. The opposite movement, the wrong movement, was called *tuathail*. It is mentioned by Sir Walter Scott as still being practised in his time, and was of special importance to protect women in childbirth or at a christening, when men would carry flaming torches in a circle round the house or church. For one suffering from tubercular diseases, his toenails and fingernails were cut, put in a bag and whirled round his head, while he chanted "deisol, deisol!"

CLOCKS

Clepsydras (literally "stealing water") were the water-clocks used by the Egyptians. Later a dial and cogwheel were introduced, so that the time could be measured in motion. These came from the Chinese and the Arabs, and were gradually introduced into Europe. (There is a striking mosaic of a Byzantine water-clock to be seen in the Church of Loaves and Fishes by the lakeside in Galilee.)

"Clockwise" is recognized as being a motion from left to right, and follows the majority pattern. There is evidence of an early Japanese clock which rotated "widdershins" (right to left) but it does not seem to have made much influence, or altered the prescribed movement.

The clockwise movement is one which has to be accepted by the left-hander, just as Greenwich Time is accepted (even by the Chinese) as the one standard in the world. It is probably the only universally accepted principle on earth.

The problem for left-handers began when the wrist-watch was developed. It was natural for the majority to wear it on the left wrist, so as to leave the right hand unencumbered, for writing.

The winder was therefore fixed so that it could be wound with the right hand only. It is, of course, possible for the left-hander to remove the watch from the wrist in order to wind it, but there has been agitation from the left-handers to produce a watch to be worn, and wound, on the *right* wrist, and, as will be seen in the references to left-handed devices, this has now been achieved by that very practical and ever watch-worthy race, the Swiss.

CURES AND SUPERSTITIONS

The rabbit's foot and the touch of the hand were probably the most popular cures. But recipes for cures were not entirely confined to the right. The famous rabbit's foot ought, it appears from many sources, to be the left hind foot. This applies to good luck as well as a cure. One formula is a little difficult to satisfy. The rabbit must be "a graveyard rabbit caught at full moon." Another creature which enjoys both popularity and unpopularity is the toad, regarded by many as one of the familiars of the witch. Yet Shakespeare wrote "The toad, ugly and venomous, hath yet a precious jewel in his head," and one John Moncrieff, who in 1731 published *The Poor*

Man's Physician, recommended the following recipe as a cure for bleeding—

"Take a Toad and dry it very well before the Sun, then put it in a linen Cloth, and hang it with a string over the part which bleedeth, and hang it so low that it may touch the Breast on the Left side, near the Heart. This will stay all bleeding at the Mouth, Nose, Wound, or anything whatsoever." Ira Wile, who discovered this recipe, adds: "little did Moncrieff guess that nearly two centuries later the toad would actually be found to contain a coagulating substance."

Although the chopping-off of the right hand was one of the favourite primeval punishments, the Cheyenne Red Indians had a "medicine" necklace which consisted of human fingers, a favoured one being *left* fingers of warriors killed in battle.

As for the Romans, who at first regarded the left hand or side as propitious—the word "sinister" had no derogatory meaning until the Augurs "took a hand"—there were many cures recommended by Pliny and others. His *Natural History* was the standard work of the day. A dead man's left hand was recommended for scrofula or throat trouble. A spider boiled in oil (after being caught with the left hand) could cure earache. Inflammation of the eyes could be cured by applying the left eye of a frog to one's own left eye, and so on. A remarkable character, Pliny, famed as the most learned man of his time.

Marcellus gave several recipes for a cure. An aching tooth on the left side could be relieved by applying a hot dried bean to the right elbow. A ring placed on the middle finger of the left hand—that celebrated finger—would cure hiccups. Gastro enteritis would be cured not, as today, by the entero-vioform tablets recommended for tourists who eat too much rich food abroad, or by Dr. Collis Browne's almost legendary preparation Chlorodyne, but by pressing the abdomen with the left thumb and chanting "*Adam bedam alam betoir alun botum.*" This, if the Marcellus cure were efficacious, would liven up the scene in the local surgery!

Finally, as a protection rather than a cure, Marcellus recommends husbands to ensure their wives' fidelity by touching them with a lizard's tail cut off with the left hand. What of the reaction of the wife? One could imagine the scene as a short playlet.

SCENE: *A Roman villa at sundown. The wife reclines on a couch listening to Ovid (on her left side, as was the Roman custom, leaving the right hand free). Enter the husband, a Senator.*

WIFE: Had a good day at the Forum?

HUSBAND: Not bad. Cicero was at it again, and stammering like mad, as usual. Who's this?

WIFE: Oh, that rather charming poet's called again. What on earth's that you've got in your hand?

HUSBAND: It's a—a lizard's tail.

WIFE: And what in the name of Jupiter are you doing carrying around a lizard's tail?

HUSBAND: Well, it's for—good luck and all that. Marcellus told me about it. He's a very knowledgeable chap, Marcellus.

WIFE: I think the gods must have made him mad.

HUSBAND: Lizard skin feels rather nice. Wouldn't you like to touch it?

WIFE: Touch it? If you bring that filthy thing near me I shall scream!

Presumably, Marcellus meant the application to be made while the wife was asleep.

DATES

The Chronology listed below may not, in its initial stages, be very accurate, but it becomes more reliable as time marches on. It may prove valuable to the left-hander who, being naturally sinistral ever since the unilateral state arose in mankind, may like to acquaint himself with some of the milestones, great and small, connected with sinistrality in earlier years.

Date	*Event*
Unknown	EVE created from left side of ADAM.
25,000 B.C.	Earliest cave drawings, many of them left-handed.
4241 B.C.	First calendar made by EGYPTIANS, regulated by sun and moon.
Circa 4000 B.C.	BRONZE AGE tools.
3400 B.C.	First writing formed, right to left (Sumerian).
Myth	CRONUS emasculates Uranus left-handedly. Aphrodite born.
Myth	SAMAEL (Hebrew, *semol*, meaning left) sits on Hebrew God's left hand, opposite Michael. Later replaced on the left by Gabriel.
1450 B.C.	Reign of AMENHOTEP III, Sun-God King of Egypt, patron of sun-worshippers.
Myth	ROMULUS wins over Remus in predicting flight of birds: founds Rome. Establishment of Augury.
Circa 890 B.C.	Left-handed EHUD the Benjamite kills King Eglon of Moab.
384–322 B.C.	Life of DEMOSTHENES, who filled his mouth with stones to cure his speech defect.
384–322 B.C.	Life of ARISTOTLE, who declared that handedness was acquired, not inherited. He educated Alexander the Great.
356–323 B.C.	ALEXANDER THE GREAT, reputably left-handed, who met a left-handed tribe on his journey to the East.
106–43 B.C.	Life of CICERO, the stammering senator and Augur.

Date	Event
A.D. 33	JESUS CHRIST relates the Parable of the sheep and the goats, shortly before the Last Supper, and sets the seal on anti-left-handedness—as reported by Matthew.
742–814	Life of CHARLEMAGNE, reputedly left-handed.
1312–77	Life of EDWARD III, reputedly left-handed.
1452–1519	Life of LEONARDO DA VINCI, greatest of the left-handed artists, and mirror-writer.
1475–1564	Life of MICHELANGELO, ambidextral artist.
1497–1543	Life of HOLBEIN the Younger, German portrait painter to the English royal court. Left-handed artist.
1646	SIR THOMAS BROWNE publishes his *Vulgar Errors*, in which the origin and reason about those "sinistrously disposed" is for the first time fully explained.
1649	KING CHARLES I executed. He had speech aphasia in youth, and stammered.
1709–84	Life of DR. SAMUEL JOHNSON, whose aphasia after a stroke led to theories that he was originally left-handed.
1758–1805	Life of LORD NELSON who lost his right arm in 1797 in the attack on Tenerife, and wrote "there can be no use in His Majesty's Navy for a left-handed Admiral." Later he learned to write left-handedly very well.
1775–1834	Life of CHARLES LAMB, stammerer and student of, among other things, witches and night-fears, including the Goat-Devil.
1832–98	Life of LEWIS CARROLL, stutterer, mirror-writer and originally, it is said, left-handed. He was certainly interested in the mirror-world.
1860	THOMAS CARLYLE lost the use of his right hand, and took up interest in left-handedness.
1888	MARTHA TURNER murdered in London's East End, by a left-hander, believed to have been "Jack the Ripper". First of many such murders.
1895	Ashanti campaign, in which BADEN-POWELL saluted a left-handed chieftain—the origin of the sinistral handshake of the Boy Scouts.
1924	KING GEORGE VI, as Duke of York, plays tennis left-handedly at the All-England Championships, Wimbledon.
1931	RAVEL's Concerto for the Left Hand has its first performance.

Date	Event
1939	MELIO BETTINA, American southpaw boxer, wins light-heavyweight world championship.
1946	JACKIE PATTERSON, Scottish southpaw boxer, wins world flyweight championship (held till 1948).
1953	CHARLES CHAPLIN plays violin left-handedly in film *Limelight*.
1954	JAROSLAV DROBNY, Czech left-handed tennis player, wins Wimbledon championship. Many subsequent sinistral victories.

DERVISHES

These members of an ancient Muslim fraternity dating back to the early Middle Ages, resembled a Christian order. Their organization began about the thirteenth century, and owed its ritual partly to the Sufis, the Mohammedan mystics who combined the orthodox principles of Islam with divine inspiration and *dhikr* ("remembering") which was a form of hypnotic control and exaltation, resulting in the famous Dance of the Dervish. This whirling motion could continue for many hours until the Dervish fell exhausted. The interesting part about the whirl of the Dervish is that it was supposed to be anti-clockwise. A recent correspondent writes from Pinner, Middlesex: "At the Albert Hall there was a group of Turkish dancers, with their crescent moon badges, and they danced 'widdershins' all the time, whereas the traditional English folk dances all went clockwise . . . ."

These were probably not authentic Dervishes, but the earlier tradition seems to persist. In Istanbul, the model Dervish dancers, rotating souvenirs go clockwise. Perhaps someone, sometime, will give a full explanation. Early seventeenth-century pictures of Dervishes show them with a spear held in the *left* hand. Curiouser and curiouser!

DYSLEXIA (WORD-BLINDNESS)

C. S. Orton defines dyslexia thus: "Inability to learn to read, which is out of harmony with the individual's general intelligence and ability to learn by other channels."

The presence of dyslexia is not new, though many of the theories and treatments are of recent date. A dyslexic or word-blind person

Dervish Whirling—widdershins

can be detected from his writing, his inversion of words, or his actions. It is said that Hans Andersen (1805–75) was a dyslexic, the evidence being partly in the notes and mis-spellings he made during his stay with Charles Dickens at Broadstairs, and in other manuscripts at the H. C. Andersen house at Odense. Certainly he was backward at school, and bullied for it. But, as an early "ugly duckling," he managed to get a university degree at Copenhagen, which started him on his career.

The discovery of the disability as such, according to Dr. Macdonald Critchley, was made about seventy years ago, and was "a notable event in medical taxonomy." From the very first, word-blindness was associated with left-handedness, as to some extent it is today. Critchley reports that in 1906 a proposal was put forward that all dyslexic children should be taught to be left-handed, so great

was the sinistral proportion, which varied between 15 per cent and
75 per cent.

"A number of educational psychologists in Britain and the U.S.
began to associate it as the product of environmental factors such as
broken homes, drunken parents, teacher-pupil hostility, absenteeism,
etc. . . . . The blame has fallen on one scapegoat after another, the
teacher, the parents, and the child . . . .

"In the recent renewal of interest in this problem, neurologists
have been in the forefront in urging an official recognition of
dyslexia."

Another alleged dyslexic was Lee Harvey Oswald, who assassinated
President Kennedy.

EARTH, ROTATION OF THE

Our world revolves, at a speed of 89,000 miles per hour, round the
sun. How does this affect man, the highest developed species on the
planet? Ira S. Wile sums up—

"The earth's movement is one universal stimulus to which man
has ever made response. It has been one of the powerful and unique
influences and forces in his development and evolution. It is undeniable that, if there were, and had been, no terrestrial rotation, man's
entire scheme of personal communal action and thought would be
different. The earth's movement has played a role in man's generic
behaviour."

The effects of rotation are dealt with in a number of different
sections of this book, such as Sun-worship and Augury. Galileo
denied, under pressure, the earth's movement. Newton proved the
Law of Gravity, without which we would not remain on earth at
all, as H. G. Wells's Man Who Could Work Miracles discovered.
Yet there is still a Flat-Earth Society, despite Kipling's exposure of
the subject in his finest short story "The Village that Voted the
Earth was Flat."

Man's present exploration of outer space and his experience of
weightlessness are another stage in his discoveries about himself and
the spinning globe on which he lives. Its importance in determining
right- and left-sidedness is implicit in many of the subjects of this
book, both scientific and superstitious.

EYE DOMINANCE

Left-handers must not assume that sinistrality ends with being left-handed. There are other parts of the body to be considered too, and the power of speech. Left-handers are usually left-footed: that is, the characteristic action is to kick a ball, first instinctively, then more expertly and powerfully, with the left foot—which explains why some famous left-handed footballers are placed on the left in the game, so that they naturally "centre" with that foot.

But there is an instinct, too, in the use of the eye. Which is the preferred eye for looking, single-eyed, through a magnifying glass, a microscope, a camera lens, or the sights of a rifle? Early theories in the U.S. argued that the "better seeing" eye compelled the preferred hand to work with it; but it is not as simple as all that. We have binocular vision, yet we have, each of us, a dominant or preferred eye for the above exercises. This was stressed by the American writer

Left-handed—left-eyed?

Beaufort Sims Parson in his examination of left-handedness in the 1920s, and has been confirmed by later authorities.

Dr. Margaret Clark made a special study of eye dominance in 1957: "Though many talk of the dominant eye, or the master eye, their meaning can vary considerably. Just as in handedness one can mean the better hand, or the preferred hand, so in eyedness, by the dominant eye can be meant either the eye with better visual acuity, that is, which can actually see better, or the preferred eye. Further, dominance can arise in binocular vision when one eye is being used by itself, or when one eye takes the leading role in fixating or sighting."

Visual acuity was apparently the only measure of dominance in early studies, with the right eye given the greater measure of superiority, and therefore regarded as the dominant one. But a test by L. Ganagan in 1933 showed that in only about half his cases was the keener eye, with better acuity, the preferred one, and he therefore considered acuity and dominance to be separate things, not correlated. They can be connected, however, if the dominant eye is the weaker one. This may set up difficulties in reading.

When both eyes are used, there is no apparent dominance. We know the test with the finger approaching the nose, or card with the hole in the centre, through which the two eyes fix on an object. When the dominant eye is closed, the viewer sees the object move: the closed non-dominant eye has no effect. The same test can be made with a pencil or finger held in front of the nose. B. Crider in 1935 tested 100 cases for ocular dominance, and found that right-eyedness varied between 55 and 90 per cent, left-eyedness from 6 to 33 per cent, and impartial eyedness from 0 to 26 per cent.

Miss Clark mentions also the Phi Test, an experiment with two lights, in which once again movement of one would determine dominance, and from the direction of movement could be determined whether it was ocular or central dominance. This test she does not recommend.

As far as eye-preference is concerned, she concludes "many people do not know their dominant eye, and while learning to use a microscope, for instance, have a period of experimenting with alternate eyes, and finally settle down to the use of one, In using a microscope, there is the possibility that it is not so much the dominance of the one eye as the suppression of the other which is of importance."

EYE, EVIL

There is a whole library of legends concerning this phenomenon, embracing many countries which have at one time or another acknowledged the power of the eye. The Book of Proverbs says "Eat not thou the bread of him that hath an evil eye," and though this superstition does not directly affect eye dominance or even the left eye, some of the superstitions, so potent in earlier years, are worth recalling.

Many of the protections against the evil eye are in the form of amulets or bracelet charms, worn by many of the primitive tribes in the pre-Christian era, the Egyptians, Phoenicians and Etruscans, and later the Greeks and Arabs. It was Plutarch who quoted the Greek augurs as seeing anything over the left shoulder as unlucky. But this was not the same thing as having evil power by means of the evil eye, a practice which Cicero described as a form of envy (*invidia*, literally looking at something closely) echoed by Sir Francis Bacon as being "the ejaculation or irradiation of the eye." Bishop Heliodorus of Thessaly, in the fourth century, openly believed in the malignant force of the evil eye. In Egypt, it was the potency of the oldest God, Ptah, whose eye "brought forth all the other Gods from his own eye." Amenhotep IV of Egypt gave his pronouncement of his power thus: "I am he, when he opens his eye it becomes light, when he closes his eye it becomes dark." He added, to his followers: "Shoot forth thine eye, that it may slay the evil conspirators."

In Morocco, the Great Feast is accompanied by protections against the evil eye. In this case, henna is the great cure, particularly among unmarried men (to whom a wrong marriage can be a curse) who daub it on the right hand and then the left—bachelors particularly include the left hand, apparently. Together with the sacred amulets, this was supposed to confer immunity from the evil eye.

Among the Moroccans, there was also the habit among the women of tying a collection of beads, shells and coins on a string above the left ankle of a mother, to protect her from the local *dijnn* or devils— and to stop any noise from the devils, a man had merely to moisten his right forefinger and place it in his right ear.

Amulets have survived to this day, and those containing a single eye can still be bought in souvenir shops by people who have never known what magical properties they were once supposed to have. They were good-luck charms. Bad luck was to be "overlooked" by the evil eye, and this is much more difficult to define, since it does not involve touching anyone, merely looking at them, a characteristic capable of many interpretations, from the really evil look to what James Thurber described as "that cold, flat look which one woman fetches another"—as evil, presumably, as any *djinn* could devise.

FISH

Fish have no hands, only fins, so they would not enter into a consideration of handedness. But as far as sidedness is concerned—and this is all to do with left and right—the fish on your fishmonger's slab show a great diversity in their habits in the water before they are caught and offered to human beings.

Deep-sea fish are all bilateral. But what of the flat-fish whose glassy eyes gaze at you at the local shop? They are known technically as *pleuronectes*. They react to the forces of light and heat, characteristics which determine their movements in shoals over the seasons, and their position when lying on the sea-bed. It has been said that they react in a similar way to colour-blind people. A list was made out by J. T. Cunningham in his *Natural History of Marketable Marine Fishes of the British Islands* in 1896. He established four types—

First, with eyes on the right side: plaice; flounder; dab, lemon dab; witch.

Eyes on left side in arctic waters: halibut; long rough dab.

Eyes on right side in Mediterranean: sole.

Eyes on left side: turbot; brill.

The eye of the flat-fish apparently travels round the head until it is uppermost, towards the light. Much depends on the depth and heat of the water in which the fish swims. The turbot normally inhabits warm waters, and its eyes and colour are on the left side. The halibut prefers colder waters, and is coloured on the right side, with the appropriate eye. The flounder is a left-sided species in tropical waters, and a right-sided species in cold arctic waters. The sole is right-eyed in Scandinavia, left-eyed in the Indian Ocean, and the Mediterranean. This can surely only be explained by the degree of light penetrating the waters in which they swim.

As for the lobster, it was the great Aristotle, no less, who noticed variations in the size of its claws. The small claw is known as the "fish" claw, the larger the "club" claw, and the lobster, of either sex, is either left or right in its use of the dominant claw. Many experts have studied its habits, particularly in the United States, and the incidence of use is, they agree, about fifty-fifty. The "club" is found either on the right or the left side of the body, and is used for crushing.

Crabs also have a claw-preference, in about equal proportions of left and right. Experiments have been made particularly with the fiddler crab, the only one of its breed which moves sideways, always in the direction of the light. Since handedness is about equal, the crab, like the lobster, does not seem to be subject to heredity, and could not therefore qualify as a Mendelian recessive.

Hermit crabs, on the other hand (or claw) are particularly dextral, and drag themselves backwards with two legs, the right of which is longer than the other.

Was it crabs and their habits which inspired T. S. Eliot to write, in "The Love Song of J. Alfred Prufrock"—

> *I should have been a pair of ragged claws*
> *Scuttling across the floors of silent seas.*

Hermit or fiddler?

FREEMASONS

A worldwide cult with secret ritual said by some to have originated with Solomon and the building of the Temple in Jerusalem. The two pillars, Jachin and Boaz, in front of the Temple, are especially important to Freemasonry. The modern Grand Lodges of England were constituted in the mid-eighteenth century (Hogarth was one of the early Masons, as was Robert Burns in Scotland).

Soon the movement—which was not Jewish—spread to Europe and America (collecting celebrities ranging from George Washington to Mozart, who composed several items of Masonic music). It was banned, however, by the Roman Catholics—as it still is—and forbidden in Spain. Many members of the British Royal Family have been Freemasons: the present Grand Master is the Duke of Gloucester.

There are 500,000 Freemasons living in Britain. Apart from dressing up in elaborate aprons and indulging in expensive banquets, Freemasons raise money for schools and hospitals and indigent persons. They are particularly powerful in the police.

What has this to do with handedness? Simply that the ritual of the Freemasons is as pro-right and anti-lefthanded as that of any Arab sect. The punishment for divulging the secret is to have the right hand cut off and slung over the left shoulder on a piece of cord—an echo of the Hand of Glory and the Black Mass—"there to wither and die." There is no record of this ever having been carried out, but it is still in the rules of the game, or whatever Freemasonry is. At the initiation of an Apprentice, he must appear before his superiors, according to the Catechism of 1776, with his left trouser leg torn open at the knee. The question is then put to him—

"When you was made an Apprentice, why was your left knee bare bent?"

The reply has to be—

"Because the left knee is the weakest part of my Body, and an Enter'd Apprentice is the weakest part of Masonry."

Freemasons' hand and finger gestures, which vary according to the day of the week, indicate the answer to the unspoken question: "Are you a Mason?"

This cult will obviously continue. It has large funds everywhere, and helps all but Catholics and presumably sinistrals—though King George VI, a left-hander, was also a high authority among the Masons. Perhaps there was a dispensation with the Grand Lodge for his valet to tear his *right* trouser leg at his initiation. But, one may ask, what happened to the trousers?

HAIRDRESSING

Can hairdressers or barbers be left-handed? Certainly there are left-handed scissors now readily available: but hair-dryers are so arranged that only the *right* thumb can be used to press the switch. To use the left is a contortion.

In 1968, a left-handed apprentice from Swindon, Wiltshire, applied for a training course in hairdressing from the Ministry of Labour in Bristol. He was provided with two pairs of left-handed

"The left knee bare bent"

scissors, and paid for six months' training. After finishing the course satisfactorily, he began to apply for jobs, and found his sinistrality a great handicap. His trainer referred to the "old-fashioned attitude towards left-handers" among the hairdressing profession. It is presumably obvious that, if a barber's shop has a row of chairs, with assistants cutting hair simultaneously with little room for manœuvre, the movements of a left-hander might prove embarrassing to his colleagues (even though barbers, unlike dentists, approach their clients from both sides of the chair).

The local Hairdressers' President declared, "I cannot imagine anyone being taught to cut left-handed. I've not seen one in twenty-two years." Mr. Robbins, the trainee, was sacked from several jobs, but boldly said "I'm too old to change. Anyway, it's the finished product that counts."

HAND, THE RED, OF ULSTER

Ulster has as its official arms "a hand gules couped on a field argent"
—that is, a red hand cut off on a white or silver background. The
O'Neill family, one of the oldest and most famous in Ireland's
history, also has the red hand on its shield, surmounting a wavy sea
containing a fish. These are all *right* hands, cut off at the wrist.
Since one of the punishments for criminals or captives in many
countries in the past was the amputation of their right hands, this
might seem to end the matter.

But my recent investigations into the history of left- and right-
handedness (on behalf of the sinistral hand) have revealed another
side to the story. According to two old legends, described to me by
an enterprising young lady at the Ulster Office in London, the hand
of Ulster was originally the *left* hand, cut off. Ulster was once called
Ulidia, and was a region ripe for conquest. Two chieftains, a Pict
and a Scot, raced across the sea to claim it. The race was neck-and-
neck (or rather hand-to-hand) for one of the chieftains, being right-
handed, severed his left hand and flung it ashore first, thus claiming
the territory.

A similar version of the story is told of the two chiefs of the
O'Neill and O'Donnell families riding up from Tyrone, and the
winner acting in the same way. This may all be dismissed as a sort
of Irish Arthurian legend, but it seems that the main body of Irish
noblemen wore the badge of the *left* hand, "couped." This was
re-established and given royal favour when, in 1611, King James of
England created the new order of baronet, 'a new dignitie between
barons and knights," ostensibly to raise money for the troops in
Ulster. The price was quoted at so much a soldier for the baronet to
pay, and worked out at the high figure of about £1,000. Two
hundred English baronets were created in 1611. Eight years later,
100 Irish baronets. In 1624, 100 baronets of Nova Scotia. Their
badge, which could be affixed to their coat of arms, was a red *left*
hand, which, according to the *Encyclopaedia Britannica*, was then the
arms of Ulster. The one exception was the baronetcy of Nova
Scotia, which adopted the right hand.

Proof of this can be seen today in the arms of a baronet. Sir Francis
Drake was dubbed a knight, but his brother and heir was made one
of the first baronets, and I have seen, above the door at Buckland

Abbey in Devon, the family home, a large left hand cut in the stone by the shield. When did the right hand take over from the left? It is hard to discover, but an old rhyme, quoted by the Irish historian Vinycombe, runs as follows—

> *The Red Hand of Ulster is a paradox quite,*
> *To baronets 'tis said to belong,*
> *If they use the left hand they are sure to be right,*
> *If they use the right hand they are wrong.*
> *For the Province, the opposite custom applies,*
> *And just the reverse is the rule:*
> *If you use the right hand you'll be right, safe and wise,*
> *If you use the left hand, you're a fool!*

What happens, then, if any O'Neill is made a baronet? The matter is probably settled, since the hand in the family arms is, as I have said, a dextral one. But the reason why the hand is cut off, and which hand it should be, may, like the traditional Irish Problem, never be settled.

It may be added, incidentally, that a well-known firm of brewers, Ind Coope's, uses the *right* red hand as their symbol.

Red Hand of Ulster. Compare with left hand of Baronetcy

HAND, THE UNCLEAN

Without a knowledgeable approach to this subject, particularly as it affects the Muslim countries in the Middle East, and other countries further east, it is impossible to interpret the prejudice against the left hand. It can be summed up, vulgarly if you like, but unmistakably by anyone who has considered the matter: which hand is instinctively used for what is known as the hygienic function and with which hand do you eat when there are no knives or forks?

Cous-cous with the Caliph

There is no point in avoiding the question, because it has had wide implications throughout the ages. Why, otherwise, should the English phrase "cack-handed" appear in the various parts of the country? Eric Partridge, in his *Dictionary of Slang*, defines "cack" as excrement. A "cack-hander" is therefore someone who uses the other hand: in this instance, in the great majority of cases, the right hand, leaving his left hand, as the hand of wisdom, glory, knowledge and power—exactly the opposite to Muslim tradition.

If, as has happened to the author, you are sitting down, on cushions, at a traditional banquet in Morocco, eating cous-cous with the Caliph of Casablanca, it is not only frightfully bad form to use your left hand, however sinistral you may be, but it is an implied insult to your host—not that a modern Moroccan would probably mind in the least, but his servants might take it amiss, when they come with silver kettles, to pour rose-water over your *right* hand before the banquet begins.

It is difficult to determine just how important and widely-implicated this practice is. The left hand has several bans upon it: it is the minority hand, and therefore to be ignored or shunned by the dextral majority. It has also the reputation of being the Unclean Hand (and this extends to the Hindu and Buddhist traditions as well as the Muslim). Furthermore, it has been identified, in most religions, with the Evil Spirit, the Powers of Darkness, the Devil, Witchcraft and what-have you. Elsewhere one can read how the Christian religion damned the left-hander; but the condemnation was not the same as the Muslim ban, which has always been more physical than mystical.

There is a whole field of social exploration here, for anyone willing to undertake the task. It has certainly had far-reaching consequences affecting the position of the sinistral in society, and the odium varies from country to country. Jesus Christ did not, according to the Pharisees, wash before dinner. "To eat with unwashen hands defileth not a man," He said to the outraged Orthodox Jews. But when it came to a choice between right and left hands, we know that, according to the disciple Matthew, Jesus condemned the left hand and preferred the right, in a choice between Hell and Heaven. How much had this to do with the Arab dislike of the left hand, not so much as the wicked but as the unclean hand?

There is obviously much more research to be done on this subject. How much is hygiene associated with holiness?

JEWISH CUSTOMS AND SAYINGS

At Succoth, the Feast of Tabernacles, worshippers wave a *lulab* (a palm branch with pieces of myrtle and willow tied on each side) in the right hand, and an *etrog* (a citrus fruit known as "Adam's apple") in the left hand. It must be to the left, since it is the evil or "forbidden" fruit of the Garden of Eden.

Tradition with burial of the dead was to place the left hand on the tomb. To quote Isaiah xlviii, 11: "For mine own sake, even for mine own sake, will I do it; for how should my name be polluted? And I will not give my glory unto another."

"When the Children of Israel perform his will, they make the right hand his left hand. When they do not perform his will, they make even the right hand his left hand." (*Pentateuch: Targum Onkelos.*)

"Is there a right and left in heaven above? This means that the intercessors stand on the right hand and the accusers on the left." (*The Midrash: Tachuma Shemoth.*)

LOBSTERS

Aristotle first drew attention to the fact, as he observed it, that the right or crushing claw was the larger and stronger. An observant member of the American Fishing Commission, Francis Herrick, noted that "the members of a brood are either right-handed or left-handed, that is, having the crushing claw on the same side of the body." He also noted the sensitivity of lobsters' eyes to the light. His researches reported 1,064 lobsters with right crushers, as against 1.266 with left crushers, and only three with both claws alike. Dr. Wile, who has made a similar kind of investigation in the U.S., has discovered a fifty-fifty ratio of right- and left-handed types.

The eyes of the lobster are mobile, and on stalks, which relieves them of the necessity for unilateral co-ordination. As for the voice, I leave the rest to Lewis Carroll—

> *'Tis the voice of the Lobster: I heard him declare,*
> *"You have baked me too brown, I must sugar my hair."*

> As a duck with its eyelids, so he with his nose
> Trims his belt and his buttons, and turns out his toes. . . .

This is after the famous "Lobster Quadrille." One wonders how much Lewis Carroll *knew* about his marine creatures.

LUCK, GOOD AND BAD

There are so many superstitions and prophecies of good and ill fortune that we can list only a few: but left-handers should be aware of them, since most of the lucky symbols are what could be termed "left-handed" compliments to them.

Salt: When spilled on the table (as Judas Iscariot is said to have done at the Last Supper) throw a pinch over the left shoulder (where the Devil sits) with the right hand.

Superstitions: Spilling the salt

Stockings: Put on the left stocking first and then the right: with shoes, first the right, then the left (Scottish and Jewish). What is the rule for pantie-hose?

Sneeze: To the right, good luck. To the left, back luck (first mention by Plutarch).

Palm of the hand. Itching in left palm, giving money away. In right palm, about to receive money (Scottish; the German meaning is the other way round).

Wine should always be served from the right, and to pass a loving cup to a neighbour *anti*-clockwise is to bring bad luck to the entire party, and to imply ill-will to the host, as a deliberate insult.

Love, to win: Not only were the usual love-potions and aphrodisiacs used. An odd Irish recipe was to write a letter "of most desperate love with a raven's quill in the blood of the ring finger of the left hand." Hardly auspicious, according to tradition.

Penis: An unusually large organ, with an abnormality on the right side, meant power and success. An unusually small one, together with some abnormality on the left side, meant weakness, disease, and failure. This has been traced back to the Babylonian-Assyrian era.

Claws and paws: In India the lion's and tiger's claws bring good luck: in Northern Asia it is the bear's paw (a familiar name for English taverns): in England and the U.S., the rabbit's or hare's foot.

Magpies: "To see three magpies on the left when on a journey is unlucky: but two on the right hand is a good omen" (Irish). In Sweden, the magpie is considered, like the raven elsewhere, a bird of ill omen. The same has been quoted in Devon.

Spittle: When you see something presaging bad luck, spit over your right shoulder three times. This applies if you meet a man with a "north eye" (a squint).

Christening: To have water sprinkled by a left-handed priest is the worst of bad luck. See Thomas Dekker, *The Honest Whore:* "I am the most wretched fellow! Sure, some left-handed priest christened me, I am so unlucky."

Husband, How to choose a: In Scotland, a maiden would cut an apple into two halves, and sit combing her hair in front of a mirror, with the apples on a table behind, to right and left. Her suitor would then appear in the mirror, and her choice would depend on which piece of apple he stole—preferably, of course, the right (though seen in a mirror it would be the left).

In the lore of the Maoris (whose habits have been studied in great detail by the French sociologist Robert Hertz) the lover first notes the direction of the wind, if he is in a boat. If the wind blows him in the direction of the loved one, "he takes a feather in his left hand, passes it under his left thigh, and then holding it upright in his out-thrust left hand, he recites his charm, which concludes with an appeal to the winds to waft hitherward the desired woman."

Note here that it is the left hand which is propitious. The Maoris, in New Zealand, live in the Southern hemisphere, where the sun rises on the left hand, if you are facing south.

When a girl is married and pregnant, records Lynn Thorndike, American author of a history of magic, "among signs to tell whether she will give birth to a boy or girl, he asks her simply to hold out her hand. If she extends the right, the child will be a boy: if the left, a girl." But if the wife knew of this superstition, she would presumably hold out her right hand, to keep him happy until the almost even-odds event of birth, with the proportion of males slightly ahead.

It was, to conclude on a slightly bizarre note, one Kiranides, King of Persia, who recommended that the testicles of a weasel, the right and the left, could be used as charms to stimulate or prevent conception. The operation is too elaborate to set out in detail, but it involved the use of the left hand, with the holder of the testicles (which must have been very easy to lose) facing East.

Hand of Glory: One of the elements of the Black Mass. The *right* hand of a criminal hanging on a gibbet would be cut off, and boiled down to extract the fat, which would then, by admixture of certain other ingredients, be made into a wax candle, coloured black, to be used at the ceremony.

Hand, applauding: It was the psychologist Alfred Adler who first drew attention to the fact that, in instinctive hand-clasping or applauding, it is the dominant hand whose thumb is uppermost. Watch any audience applauding, and you can tell which are the left-handers.

Henna: Much used in the Middle East as a protection against the evil eye. Not used by married men, but bachelors (presumably partly as a protection against marrying a woman with the evil eye) apply it to the right hand.

Ear: Ear-charm by Cornelius Agrippa; "Whisper the words 'gaspar fyrt myrrhum, Melchior, Balthasar aurum' into the right ear of a man suffering from the falling sickness [epilepsy[and he will recover within an hour." In Ireland, if the right ear tingled, it meant you were being praised, and vice versa.

Bees, charm for swarming: "Take earth, throw it from under thy right foot with thy right hand and say—

> *'I take it under foot, I have found it.*
> *Verily earth avails against every creature.*
> *And against mischief and mindlessness,*
> *And against the great tongue of man.'* "

To be "the bee's knees" (U.S. slang, 1920s) was to be not only beautiful but fortunate.

Cat, black: A lucky symbol, particularly if it cross your path, and more especially if you see one on your wedding day. There is apparently no particular left-right movement involved, though the cat has erroneously been credited with leading by the right paw when walking, an unusual habit for quadrupeds.

Foot and Leg: Similar luck symbols to those under *Stockings.* Pliny reports that the Emperor Augustus "put his left shoe for his right" on one occasion, and was nearly killed by his own soldiers, who were demanding a wage increase. It was, apparently, generally held for centuries that to put a shoe on the wrong foot was to court disaster. Lewis Carroll may well have been thinking of this when he wrote of those who

> *madly squeeze a right-hand foot*
> *Into a left-hand shoe*

in his poem of the old man sitting on a gate. The Muslims made it a rule to put on and take off the right shoe before the left.

Leg movements were equally lucky or unlucky. "Getting out of bed the wrong side" is a familiar one. It involved rising anti-clockwise, thus putting the left foot out of bed first. In Scottish lore, the phrase "first footing" is still in familiar use. On any occasion, it was unlucky to cross a threshold with the left foot or "keir" foot: particularly so at New Year, on the traditional visits to neighbours' houses, or when carrying a newly-wed bride into the matrimonial home. This was noted by Dr. Johnson and Sir Walter Scott in later years.

The Muslims had a similar preference for entering a house with the right foot: but if the house were suspect of being haunted by a *djinn*, or evil spirit, then it was more auspicious to enter with the *left* foot, to appease the evil one—a rare form of appeasement, for Muslims.

MARRIAGE

Eve was created from a rib on Adam's left side, so 'tis said, though Sir Thomas Browne added: "I dispute it not: because I stand not assured which is the right side of a man, or whether there be such a distinction in nature."

Marriages are full of superstitions and luck symbols, from chimney-sweeps and black cats and bridesmaids avoiding green dresses to the dipping of right hands in the blood of goats and sheep, to ward off the evil eye, and the drinking of milk, being a white substance, and white being a colour of good fortune in many countries. In Ireland, if a man, at his marriage, unbuttoned one button of his breeches at the right knee, he could never be harmed by the fairies or the "little people." In Scotland, it was the buckle and latchet of the bridegroom's *left* shoe which was to be undone, to keep away the witches.

Every country has its marriage customs. In Britain and the U.S., the bride stands on the groom's left side, as befits the weaker or feminine side, and the ring is placed on the third finger of the left hand: this is the "heart" finger, the one which is supposed to be closest to the human heart.

On the Continent, the ring is placed on the right hand—perhaps in acknowledgement of its dominance. The distinction is quite clear. Indeed, on one occasion when Queen Elizabeth II of Britain paid a state visit to Paris, she appeared there with her wedding ring transferred to her right hand—and in a monarch so meticulous in protocol one can only believe that this was a deliberate compliment to her hosts, the French.

MARRIAGE, MORGANATIC

The origins of this *mariage à main gauche*, as it is called in French (another insult to the sinistrals), apparently derives from Germany, although it is found in the royal houses of other European countries. The "wife," if not of equal rank or status to the husband, is not entitled to right of succession, property or title. This last proviso proved of importance during the crisis over the proposed marriage between King Edward VIII and Mrs. Simpson in 1936. Under the Royal Marriage Act of 1772, no descendant of King George II could marry without the consent of the monarch: but Edward, later Duke of Windsor, was himself the monarch. One of the proposals put forward then was that of morganatic marriage, which was legal, but would preclude Mrs. Simpson from being called Queen Wallis.

The term "morganatic," applied generally to one of royal blood marrying a person of inferior rank, comes from the Latin *matrimoniam ad morganaticum*, and refers to the German *Morgengabe*, the morning gift presented on the wedding day by the bridegroom to the bride. As in the French version, this is performed *zur linken Hand* and the groom presented the left hand to his wife.

Such marriages were recognized as fully binding by the Church, and the children were not illegitimate or "sinister"; no other later marriage was valid during the lifetime of the contracting parties.

In England, King George IV's marriage to Mrs. Fitzherbert was in the morganatic manner. It has not, however, been an issue since the Windsor *affaire* in 1936, though on her marriage with Prince Hugo Carlos of Spain, Princess Irene of the Netherlands had to renounce her right of succession to the throne.

MENDELIAN RECESSIVE

If a left-hander finds himself described as one of these, he need not worry unduly: but he should first be armed with the facts, in order to give the answer.

Gregor Johann Mendel (1822–84), an Austrian biologist, was of peasant parentage. Nevertheless he took his degree at Vienna University, and became a priest at an Augustinian monastery at Brünn in 1843. For fifteen years he taught natural history in the monastery school, and from 1860 until his death he was Abbot. His valuable experiments on heredity were made in the monastery

You're nothing but a Mendelian Recessive!

garden, upon sweet and edible peas, a strange medium, one might think, for such an important subject. The results were not published until 1900, but they were far-reaching, extending to the realms of man.

It was the Mendelian "ratio" which many experts believe made the right-hander the dominant, as opposed to the recessive man, and this did not apply only to the physical actions of the majority, but to physiological and social pressures on the minority. This is no place to discuss the whole complexity of Mendel's laws, but it is certainly apparent that, with the gradual emergence of thought and choice in man, the difference between the use of the two hands became a matter of importance, with the right predominant.

"Il faut cultiver notre jardin," wrote Voltaire in *Candide*. Mendel certainly cultivated his, making it as famous as the Garden of Eden, with edible peas instead of an apple.

All things memorable and important can be summed up in a Nursery Rhyme, and since this subject arises even before the nursery, the following may explain the situation—

Sing a song of Mendel
(Peas in a pod)
Four and twenty chromosomes
Packed in a bod.
When the bod was opened
Results were most impressive:
The babe was either dominant
Or else it was recessive.

MOLECULES (STEREO–ISOMERS)

According to Martin Gardner in his *Ambidextrous Universe*, there are molecules which are a non-symmetrical structure of atoms. This was first discovered in the early nineteenth century by the French physicist Jean-Baptiste Biot, and his discovery was confirmed by the great Louis Pasteur, experimenting on crystals of tartaric acid. When he saw the crystals of opposite handedness in operation as mirror-images, says Gardner, he was so overcome with emotion that he rushed from his laboratory, shouting to a colleague, "I have just made a great discovery . . . I am so happy that I am shaking all over!" He sought out Biot and repeated the experiment before him. Again, there was a strong "levo-motion" (movement to the left). Biot said, "My dear son, I have loved science so deeply that this stirs my heart." Other scientists carried experiments a stage further until it was definitely established that right- and left-handedness existed among certain molecules. So, if a sugar is called dextrose (this applies to table sugar) it is polarized to the right. If it is called levulose (fruit sugar) it is just the opposite.

"Stereo-isomer" is the name applied to these non-symmetrical molecules.

MOLES

One would not have thought that a whole galaxy of luck symbols would have arisen from the presence of these harmless blemishes on the body. But students of witchcraft will know that one of the signs of the Devil was a mark on a certain part of the body, and one of the more obscene acts of a witch-trial was the examination, in public, of the accused woman's naked body, for proof of her attachment to the Devil.

Dr. Ira S. Wile had collected a vintage assortment on the interpretations of moles. Here is a summary (and look at yourself carefully in a mirror one day, to see if you qualify) taken from works by John Brand in *Popular Antiquities* (London, 1842) and Ashwell Stoddart's *Treatise on Moles* (New York, 1805).

Moles on the right arm and shoulders denote great wisdom: on the left debate and contention. A mole on the right side of the forehead is a sign of great riches to men and women: on the other side, quite the contrary. Moles on the ear have the same contrary significance.

A mole on the left knee signifies riches and virtue; if on a woman's left knee, many children. If a man has a mole on a place near the heart, it doth denote him undoubtedly wicked.

When there is a mole on the left corner of an eye, the person having that mole is subject to melancholy and the diseases that proceed therefrom.

A mole on the left side denotes a luxurious person. On the left belly, it denotes affliction. On the right side it betokens good fortune.

A mole on the left buttock signifies that trouble may be lurking nearby. A mole on a knuckle bone means good luck. So does a mole on the right side of the groin. So on the right thigh and the right cheek, and so on—the recital becomes monotonous, with the good-luck emphasis always to the right, and no exceptions.

There have been prints made of the human body, depicting the exact position and meaning of the blemishes. They certainly came in very useful for the witch-hunters, if any blemish could be found on the left side, while these cruel, sadistic men went about their work, which was more akin to the devil's side than anything except perhaps Hitler's Gestapo.

MOLLUSCS

Most spiral shells curve to the right when the aperture is to the right. But there are examples of shells with an opposite twist. That sharp-minded and ingenious author Jules Verne, in his *Twenty Thousand Leagues under the Sea*, refers to a shell which turned from left to right, and more recently, in England, there was the case of a "left-handed" whelk getting into the news and on to the radio. There were doubts as to the proportion of "left-hand" whelks or snails—certainly, said one expert, not more than one in a million. The peculiarity was also held to be hereditary and not, as had previously been believed, due to a disturbance in the embryo of the shell, such as might produce a pearl in a bivalve oyster. Today, there is a restaurant in Brighton called "The Left-Handed Whelk."

Dr. Wile, a great authority on marine life, declares that the degree of light penetrating the water has much to do with movement and sidedness, and that molluscs which are liable to be sinistral or dextro-sinistral are either land or fresh-water shells, as opposed to rarity in salt-water shells.

MUSIC

The most famous left-hander in the history of music was not King David, who played the harp, and was a member of the partly-sinistral tribe of Benjamin, but C. P. E. Bach, one of the sons of J. S. Bach, who played only the clavichord and organ because he was "impeded" with other instruments, according to *Grove's Dictionary of Music and Musicians*.

With a stringed instrument such as the violin, the strings have to be "switched" (as they were when Charles Chaplin played in his film *Limelight*) and the bridge bar inside the case moved to the opposite side. The same is true of a guitar, such as played by Paul McCartney, a left-handed Beatle. The harp that once echoed through the famous comedies of the Marx Brothers was on the opposite shoulder of the late, left-handed Harpo Marx, who, in his autobiography never once mentions his sinistrality.

Piano concertos for the left hand only (all composed for people who had lost the use of the right hand, not for natural sinistrals) have been composed by Ravel, Prokoviev and Britten. There are no concertos for the right hand only: musically, this is well-nigh impossible.

The recorder, with its finger-stop, is said to be more easy to play for a left-hander.

The piano presents no dextro-sinistral problems. Left and right hand work in harmony. But it is noticeable that the left hand bears the brunt of the bass clef. Musical history indicates that it is well-nigh impossible to compose a piano sonata or concerto for the right hand, but it is possible for the left hand solo. Paul Wittgenstein was an Austrian pianist who lost his right hand during the first world war. One of his friends was the Basque composer Maurice Ravel, who composed for him a concerto for the left hand alone. It was one of Ravel's last works, and not one of his best—Wittgenstein found it almost impossible to play the solo part, and later another pianist had to take his place.

But Ravel wrote on the score: "This is not so much to show what the left hand can do, but to prove what can be done for the appendage which suffers from sinistral stigma."

Benjamin Britten's concerto was written to encourage the pianist Harriet Cohen, who had seriously injured her right hand, and seemed unable to play again. This was a psychological touch. So too, was the case of the pianist Cyril Smith, who suffered a stroke and lost the use of his left hand. Knowing that no composer would attempt a dextral concerto, he combined forces with his pianist wife Phyllis Sellick in a successful threesome— two of hers, one of his. He describes this in his book, *Concerto for Three Hands*.

*Many guitarists, like Paul McCartney,
have sinistrally-strung guitars*

Musical instruments are not much affected by handedness, except the violin, mandoline, harp, and chromatic harmonica.

Modern left-handed players include Charles Chaplin (as mentioned above), Cole Porter, Johnnie Dankworth and two out of the four Beatles, Paul McCartney and Ringo Starr.

NIGERIANS

Though there is not any handed problem among the peoples of the Niger Delta, it has already been mentioned that the younger son of the Chief Enaharo is known to be left-handed.

The handed characteristics in the Ibo tribe were described many years ago by Arthur Leonard in his book dated 1906.

"The law among the Ibo and natives of Brass is that women are on no account to touch the faces of their husbands with the left hand, neither are they permitted to eat food or handle it with any hand other than the right. But among the Ibo and other tribes, the privilege of drinking with the left hand is only extended to experienced warriors who have killed men in war with their own hands."

This seems to be a custom peculiar to the Ibo tribe. It does not apparently apply to the rest of the tribes in the Niger Delta.

OATH, TAKING THE

"Oath" is an Anglo-Saxon word (*ath* or *eath*). The taking of oaths in the name of the Hebrew God Jehovah dates back to the days of Ezekiel and Daniel, and the oath was taken by raising the hand to heaven: almost certainly *yamin*, the right hand. Oaths were also sworn before God in the New Testament, the Book of Common Prayer ("I swear by Almighty God," etc.) and by Hamlet.

The corporal oath came later. It is referred to by that eminent lawyer Lord Justice Coke, who in 1681 declared "It is called a corporal oath, because he toucheth with his hand some part of the Holy Scripture." He does not specify which hand, but the tradition grew up unwarrantably, that the action of touching or raising the book should be done with the *right* hand. It has, the left-hander will be glad to hear, no justification in law. The Oaths Act of 1888, moreover, admitted Affirmation (without the Bible) for those who professed no religious belief, and no hand was involved.

The Oaths Act of 1909 repeats the Coke formula—

"The person taking the Oath shall take the New Testament, or in the case of a Jew, the Old Testament, *in his uplifted hand* (our italics) and shall say or repeat after the officer administering the Oath, the words, 'I swear by Almighty God,' etc."

Obviously, if a solemn oath is to be given by professing Christians, and the right hand is ordered to be used, then it follows that the right hand is admitted, by law, to be the superior hand, and the hand of truth.

Those who have been defendants on oath will be aware that the Clerk of the Court usually asks the defendant to take the book dextrally. Well, anything for a quiet life—like eating cous-cous with a caliph—but it is presumptious of the right-hander to assume that there is any legal justification for it, and if Christian custom and morals be the backbone of law, the left-hander need not regard his dextral oath to be binding.

10

Taking the Oath

This may, as with the Trial of Alice in Wonderland, be regarded as "important" or "unimportant" (the King kept on trying which word sounded best) but it is a reminder to dextrals not to assume superiority over sinistrals, in the name of Justice.

ORIGINS OF HANDEDNESS

This is one of the most important questions a left-hander may have to face. "Why did some of you have to be left-handed?" The implication by a right-hander is often that a sinistral is a freak of nature, one of God's mistakes, or, worse still, just a deliberate non-conformist in society.

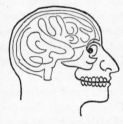

The left-hander must be versed in the various theories about the adoption of the *right* hand by the majority. This is no mere sign of superiority, but a variation of nature for which neither the right-hander nor the left-hander is directly responsible.

There are many authorities clamouring to give their views, from Thomas Carlyle, who thought dextrality began in primitive warfare, to protect the heart, to Professor Alexander Buchanan of Glasgow, who in the same century ascribed it to the greater weight of liver and lungs on the right side. Later experts, such as Dr. Abram Blau of the U.S., considered left-handedness to be a recessive element caused by emotional or physical upset (see MENDELIAN RECESSIVE).

The conflicting theories may be summed up into those which attribute left-handedness to habit and upbringing, assuming that every left-hander could easily be switched to right-handedness, which is possible and even feasible in infancy, but which scarcely ever invades such instinctive physical actions as kicking or throwing, and those who claim left-handedness, as did Sir Thomas Browne in 1648, and later Dr. D. J. Cunningham, in 1902, as "a transmitted function of the brain," generated at birth and not the result of habit and education.

"Was I born or made?" is a question every left-hander has to ask himself, and today "born" is the recommended answer. In other words, though it may appear that there are more natural left-handers in Britain and the United States and Israel than in, say, the

Soviet Union or India or the Middle East, this is simply because left-handedness is permitted almost everywhere in the former, and restricted in the latter—except in natural (and therefore significant) activities such as sport. The fact is that you cannot totally *eliminate* left-handed tendencies in anyone. Sinistrality breaks through somewhere, whatever they decree in schools and at dinner tables and in giving salutes. The Soviet Union has not suppressed its two top lawn-tennis players, nor its sinistral Olympic Gold Medallists. The incidence of left-handedness at birth is held by most authorities to be a constant, whatever social laws may compel the minority to conform to the outward behaviour of the majority, in the schoolroom, at the dining table and in the workshop. On the sports field it has seldom been insisted on, if the sinistral shows signs, as he or she so often does, of being a champion, or at any rate a cause of upset to the opponents. There is said to be one school in the south of England which encourages its cricket team to become left-handed—just to be an additional trouble to its opponents.

Sir Thomas Browne asserted long ago that right hand preference "hath no regular or certain root in nature." Our ancestors the apes were ambidextral, as were a large proportion of early primitive men, a fact proven by the discovery of early tools for left-handed use. As the brain of man increased in perception and selection, obviously the will of the majority-brain became imposed on the tribe. In the bronze age a tool became a precious possession, and would be fashioned, perhaps, for use by one hand only—usually the right hand.

From these primitive manual beginnings there arose a divergence in thought about right- and left-handedness. As Ira S. Wile describes it: "Physiological right-handed dominance would become common and the idea of left-handedness would connote danger—and possibly hazard. Through the aeons of barbarian years, passing into the customs of primitive peoples, the distinction of hands grew in force and significance, the right hand ever gaining in social preeminence . . . .

"One cannot be dogmatic in assuming that the right-handed preferential dominance was a matter of necessity, convenience, social adjustment, religious mandate or survival compulsion . . . righthandedness came to be a predominant human characteristic and

The "Genes"

finally shifted from physical non-selection to physiological domination in harmony with the Mendelian ratio . . . . There arose now, not so much a decline in the hereditary presence of left-handedness but rather a suppression of it under the demand for adaptation to changing principles of social organization, preservation, and advancement."

Left-handers of the world, you have been warned. Look to your natural origins, and assert your—well, the only English word, alas, is "rights."

Dr. Margaret Clark adds this important note on heredity, in her book on the teaching of left-handed children—

"One's chances of being left-handed are greater if there are instances of left-handedness in the family. Few would deny, however, that factors other than genetic help to determine whether any particular individual will be right or left-handed: the actual society in which he lives, and its attitude to left-handedness, other environmental factors, temperamental differences, and so on, all play a part in determining whether latent left-handedness will be cultivated or suppressed. These factors will probably have their greatest effect on the intermediates, assuming left-handedness to be a quantitative trait. The increase in apparent left-handedness in the last generation, and also the fact that so many institutions, schools and clinics make a note of the handedness of entrants, should assist geneticists in their attempts to determine the actual hereditary mechanism of hand preference."

POCKETS

At first the pocket may seem to have little to do with handedness. In fact, it is the Roman origin of the word "sinister". The Roman toga had one pocket, on the left, and the word was *siniis*, the "pocket side." This became incorporated in the name for the left side of a shield, as opposed to *dexter*. It did not have any derogatory meaning until the prophetic Augurs started their divination. The Latin word for a left-hander was *scaevola*, a diminutive of *scaevus*, which meant "towards the left side."

Through the centuries, customs have altered, and with the superstition that it is bad luck to give away money with the left hand, the money-carrying pocket changed to the right.

A left-handed gentleman, asked "In which pocket do you keep your loose change?" should be able to reply "the left side." But once again the ever-watchful Cyril Burt notes this about habits: "A friend tells me that during a long journey abroad, when apparently his wardrobe was limited, he tore a large hole, which he omitted to mend, in the right-hand pocket of his trousers. He therefore developed a habit of keeping his money in the left-hand pocket; and the habit has persisted, so that for this particular purpose he is still left-handed. His efforts to return to the more convenient pocket have only caused an irritating indecision, and have been abandoned."

PROPORTIONS OF HANDEDNESS

This is a vital question for the left-hander to be well-informed about.

"Left-handed? There can't be many
of you like that, can there?"

The right-hander may say (off-handedly, as it were) "But there are so few of you—surely only about 2 per cent. That's remarkable!"

It's not remarkable, and it's not only 2 per cent. Moreover, if you ask a right-hander to keep a look out for left-handers in his ordinary daily life, he suddenly sees them everywhere. He realizes his secretary is left-handed, he finds he has a left-handed relation, he notices people writing left-handedly in banks and post offices. You have opened for him a new world, in which the apparently insignificant minority assumes some degree of importance, and, in some situations, suffers certain disadvantages in a world apparently made for righters to live and work and fight in.

There is no average figure for the world proportion of sinistrals. Most estimates come from special surveys undertaken over the last sixty years or so, when interest began to develop in the subject of hand preference.

A left-hander may regard the *Encyclopaedia Britannica*, which has at last, in the latest edition, included a paragraph on left-handedness, to be the ultimate authority. In this, the estimate is "about 8 per cent," but the article does not quote how this figure has been reached.

Surveys have to be based on individual inquiry, not mere observation, since a large proportion of natural left-handers have been "switched" to right-handed writing in schools, and many sinistrals develop a certain amount of ambidextrality or dextrality in their habitual actions.

Ira S. Wile, an American doctor, prepared a table of estimates during his prodigious inquiries into handedness, published in Boston in 1934. Dr. Wile studied the whole subject of handedness to a degree never equalled, and all left-handers must be indebted to his investigations.

The variations climb from 1 per cent to over 30 per cent. The main challenge for a higher bracket came from Dr. Bryng Bryngelson of Minnesota, who declared "If there were no interference on the part of teachers, 34 out of every 100 children born today would become left-handed."

Wile prepared a long list of accumulating proportions among left-handers. Here is a selection from his findings—

%
1·00   Hasse & Dehner, Germany. Based on examination of 5,141 German soldiers, 1914.

2·00   James Mark Baldwin, New York, 1911.

3·80   Kasputin, Stuttgart, 1932. Based on experiments on children.

4·00   Lombroso, Cesare, 1903. A very anti-left-handed writer. No inquiry noted.

4·00   Stier, E., 1909. He earlier investigated the handedness of soldiers in the German army.

4·00   W. G. Wiseley, Ohio. Study of 18,000 pupils in Ohio School 8, 1930.

4·60   Schafer, Berlin schoolchildren, 1932.

5·10   Burt, Sir Cyril. Test in London County Council, 1921.

7·77   Schiller, Maria. Tests on 7,000 schoolchildren of Stuttgart.

7·90   Schwerz, Franz. 1,000 children in Schaffhausen, Switzerland, 1932.

11·00 Arnstein, E., 1931. 2,000 Palestinian children (this proportion seems very high).

15·70 Ramaley, Francis. Investigation of 1,000 American children.

26·10 Quinan, 1930. 1,000 university students in the U.S.

28·80 Woo and Pearson. 7,000 cases investigated in the U.S. in 1927.

29·70 Beaufort Parson, author of the American book on left-handedness, New York, 1924. He based his figure on about 800 cases of eyedness.

25·30 Dr. Ira S. Wile, 1932, based on natural carrying practices by human beings. This figure coincides with the proportion envisaged by Dr. Bryng Bryngelson.

RATS

As in so many other spheres, this animal has been very valuable in experiments relating to human behaviour: none more so than in handedness (or pawedness). Tests showed that about 80 per cent of rats are right-pawed, using this paw for reaching food, and in many other activities.

An operation removing part of one hemisphere of the brain ("making a lesion," in medical terms) made a contra-lateral paw-preference. This was an important discovery. Experts say that the operation proved there was laterality in animals without speech, and that the same operation, performed on a left-handed man, would automatically make him right-handed, and dextral in every way. It is perhaps fortunate that the discovery was not made in days when left-handers were under suspicion, as being connected with the devil and witchcraft, but in more tolerant times. There might have been wholesale physical switching, in the name of God and conformity!

The experiment disposed of the theory that handedness was acquired and not hereditary.

ROYALTY

"Uneasy lies the head," as Shakespeare wrote, "that wears a crown": and a cat may look at a king. Not only a cat, but the king's courtiers and public. Every movement and every characteristic are noted, both by his subjects and by foreigners. True, his eccentricities or peculiarities were usually condoned or explained away, and he would be called Charles the Fat, or Henry the Good, or Ivan the Terrible, or Ethelred the Unready, or whatever nickname the people liked to pin on him.

There has never, as far as is known, been a ruler called, say, Leofric the Left-hander. Yet tradition has held that many monarchs have been sinistral, and that the characteristic has been handed down through the generations, as in the House of Guelph (Windsor) where Queen Victoria, who was ambidextral, had as great-grandson King George VI, definitely left-handed, and great-great-great-grandson Prince Charles, "shifted" to the right in infancy, but left-handed in several instinctive actions.

It is presumably more important for kings and queens and presidents and other rulers to conform to the majority practice of the dextrals—at least where such matters as signing of treaties and such is concerned. A classic case is that of King Henry III, whose stroke, towards the end of his life, caused him to lose the use of his hand, so that he could not write. The hand was not specified. But in 1953, when his death-mask was discovered at Westminster Abbey, the mouth was twisted on the *right* side, indicating that the stroke occurred on that side of the brain, which would paralyse the opposite hand.

SCISSORS

These cutting instruments date back to the Bronze Age, and the spring-type was commonly used in Europe until the Middle Ages. The modern pivot-type was used in Ancient Rome, in China and Japan. In Europe, scissors date back to the sixteenth century, but mass-production only began in Sheffield, in 1761, when one Robert Hinchcliffe first used cast-steel for their manufacture.

The blades are so made that the cutting edges face each other. This, until recently, was the unkindest cut of all for the sinistral, since the cutting edges were intended for the right-handed only. Substances like paper can, perhaps, be cut with either hand, but for thicker substance such as cloth, the left-hander is helpless with a right-handed pair of scissors. It has always been difficult for a tailor to be left-handed (as with a tinker, soldier or sailor for that matter). Since most left-handers are able to acquire a certain degree of ambidextrality, this disability can partly be overcome, but only in recent years have left-handed scissors been available to the public. The sinistral pinking-shears, so essential for cutting cloth, are even more rare, and some tailors have been forced to buy two pairs, fitting the opposite parts together.

SEWING MACHINES

Is the sewing machine, like the typewriter, primarily a left-handed instrument? True, in the old machines, the handle was on the right side and could not be operated sinistrally (this had to be done by the foot, with a treadle) but the material was, and still can be, fed through the needle with the left hand, a more sensitive operation.

It is assumed by many that the sewing machine was invented by Isaac Merritt Singer (1811–75) of New York, who later settled in England. But since the mid-eighteenth century there had been many attempts at such a device: Singer's patent (which was hotly disputed by an Elias Howe of Massachusetts) was merely the final stage. With the advent of the electric machine, the question of handedness ceased, but there has been a strong rumour that Singer himself was a left-handed man. It is not for the author to stray further into a province which is mainly on the distaff side, any more than it is to decide which is the hand that rocks the cradle, or even rules the world.

SLANG TERMS

Every language has its slang phrases and regional *argot*. One of the richest and most varied is the language of Britain, and one of the most frequently nicknamed is the left-hander, the "odd man out," on whom has been heaped, through the ages, an astonishing catalogue of epithets, ranging from the derisive to the downright insulting.

In a massive and as yet unfinished work on regional dialects, Professor Orton and a team of researchers have combed the woods, and have come up with a profusion of phrases for left-handedness, many of them deriving from the same root. They usually suggest weakness or clumsiness, as does the French word *gauche*, and the Italian *mancino*, which has even more evil connotations. The Irish *kithogue* (which is also found in the Isle of Man as *kittagh*) is matched by the Scottish *keir-pawed*, and Scotland also has *gawk-handed*; the word "gawk" meaning a cuckoo or a fool. It survives in the common adjective "gawky," meaning awkward.

Variations are *dawky-handed*, which has been traced to Yorkshire, and *cork-handed*, in Derbyshire. *Clicky-handed* can be found in Cornwall, and, according to Dr. A. L. Rowse, the historian, comes from the ancient Cornish word *cledhec*. This brings us to one of the most popular phrases, particularly common in the north of England—*cack-handed*, which is almost the British equivalent of the American "southpaw," but for a very different reason. Eric Partridge, that expert on British slang, declares that the word "cack" means excrement. The implications of this are obvious—or would be to a Muslim, to whom the left hand is the unclean one (see HAND, THE UNCLEAN). We are therefore left with an explanation other than that of mere clumsiness: but what is the connexion, say, between Liverpool and Libya, in this attitude to the left-hander? Does uncleanness come into the matter, or is the British word merely derisive?

More bizarre phrases, of uncertain origin, are *ballock-handed* (Yorkshire), *keggy-handed* (Birmingham), *dawky-handed* (Leeds), *scrammy-handed* (Bristol), *coochy-handed* (Dorset), *bang-handed* (Lancashire), *cuddy-handed* (Teesdale), *spuddy-handed* (Gloucestershire), *squippy-handed* (Wiltshire).

In Sheffield, you can apparently be *dolly-pawed*, the word "dolly" meaning weak or soft. This has a surprising echo in Australia, where left-handers are often described as *molly-dukers*, the word "duke" meaning hand, and "molly" meaning weak. (This would not seem to apply to some of Australia's leading athletes and sportsmen.)

So the catalogue goes on: you can be a *cuddy-wifter* in the north, and *Marlborough-handed* in the south. (The latter is a very difficult definition to determine). You can be *wacky-handed* in the Midlands, and *bawky-handed* again in the North. The astonishing thing is, that in this very authoritative list compiled by Professor Orton, opposite the phrase "right-handed," in each case, there is only one word, i.e. "right-handed." All the wacky and squiffy and gawky phrases are heaped on the hapless sinistral. It is merely a measure of the contempt felt by a majority towards a minority.

Orton's full list is as follows—

Southern Counties
- Back(handed)
- Cam
- Gammy
- Kack
- Keggy
- Marlborough
- Scrammy
- Skiffle
- Skivver
- Watty
- Click
- Skiffy
- Coochy
- Scoochy
- Scroochy
- Squiffy
- Squippy

"Coochy-handed" (Devon)

Six Northern counties and Isle of Man
- Bang(handed)
- Kittagh
- Ballock
- Bang
- Bawky
- Cowey
- Cowley
- Cuddy
- Dollock
- Gallock
- Gally
- Gammy
- Gawky
- Gawp
- Golly
- Kack
- Keggy
- Gar-pawed

"Bang-handed"
(Tyne-Tees area)

Cow-pawed
South-pawed
Cuddy-wifter
Kay-pawed
Kittaghy

"*Kithogue*" *(Ireland)*

SPORT
Baseball

In his illustrated book on Left-handers, the American author James
T. de Kay has included the following interesting observations about
baseball.

"The left-handed batter," he writes, "faces the first base when he
has completed his swing, and so he has a head start in running out
his hit. 32 per cent of all major League batters are left-handed. A
left-handed pitcher can keep an eye on first base during his wind-up,
and so cut down a runner's lead. 30 per cent of all major league
pitchers are southpaws.

"The left-handed first baseman can cover a tremendous area of
the infield with his right (gloved) hand. Also, he's got an advantage
throwing to second for the double play. 48 per cent of all major
league first basemen are left-handed. But there are absolutely no
left-handed catchers!"

Perhaps the great Babe Ruth, left-hander, started it all. His mantle
has certainly fallen on players like Mantle, and others. The term
"southpaw" is, incidentally, originally derived from baseball, not
from boxing, where it mainly belongs today. At Chicago's West
Side stadium the left-handed batter faced south.

Boxing

The word "southpaw" is so often given to a left-handed boxer that one might be forgiven for thinking that it originated in this sport, instead of in Baseball. Webster's *International Dictionary* gives definitions for both sports.

Fisticuffs—boxing without rules—has obviously been the prerogative of man since time began. Roman gladiators boxed, but with the cruel *caestus*, a sort of knuckle-duster bound with leather. The favourites of the Prince Regent boxed bare-fisted. But always the "southpaw" was the man to look out for, and still is. He leads with the right, and his main punch is with the left. He also leads with the right foot, and footwork is an important element in boxing.

Southpaw boxers have had their successes, but it is estimated that only about ten of them have ever won World Championships—and the World Heavyweight has never been won by a southpaw. The most famous names are Freddie Miller, World Featherweight Champion from Cincinnati; Melio Bettina, Italo-American light-heavyweight (1939); Jimmy Carruthers of Australia, Bantamweight World Champion; and the Scotsman, Jackie Patterson, Flyweight World Champion in 1946.

Cricket

In 1909, two left-handed Australian batsmen were among the team which visited England for the Test series—Warren Bardsley and V. S. Ransford. Both were outstanding successes. In the final game at the Oval, London, Bardsley made two separate centuries, a feat never achieved before in Test cricket by an Australian.

At the turn of the century, Yorkshire was the dominant team in the championship, thanks largely to the left-handed bowling of the almost legendary figure of Wilfred Rhodes, perhaps the greatest bowler England has ever had.

There have been so many champion cricketers who are left-handed that it is invidious to name any of them above their sinistral peers. It is perhaps sufficient in recent years to recall that left-handed Brian Close of Yorkshire was Captain of England in 1968, and that in the Test series between Australia and the West Indies in 1969, both captains were left-handers—Bill Lawry and Gary Sobers (the most remarkable cricketer of modern times, whose personal opinions on his left-handedness are of interest).

There is, obviously, from the batting point of view, an advantage in having a left-hander in the side. Sir Henry Newbolt wrote—

> *There's a breathless hush in the Close tonight:*
> *Ten to make, and the match to win* . . . .

In many such a situation, when the voice of a schoolboy "rallied the ranks," a team might be glad they had a left-hander left, for whenever he faces the bowler, the opposing team has to change position, and one of the umpires has to move over, and this is, in cricket, not an operation which can take place quickly. The statuesque stride of the team has to be taken into account. It is therefore of interest to know that cricket teams, like baseball teams, can take advantage of this sinistrality among their members. This does not, of course, affect the actual ability of the left-handed batsman: it is merely a matter of gamesmanship in cricket, a sport normally so decorous that even when there are riots on the field in many different places, the announcement "Tea Taken," on the newspaper cables is enough to calm the outside world. Everything, right or left-handed, stops for tea, but there is this way of holding up proceedings, which is perfectly legal according to the rules of the game. As far as is known, no objection has been taken against a left-hander because he is a left-hander, and this is also true of baseball, where it may be very wise for a captain to put a "southpaw" striker in, about seventh or eighth in the line.

Fencing

This noble art, which reached its peak in Italy about the seventeenth century, with elaborately chased weapons, has always admitted the true left-hander to its adherents. Indeed, the presence of the "southpaw" can be traced back to Roman days. He was much in demand for gladiatorial combats. Indeed, one un-named historian asserted that 50 per cent of gladiators were sinistral, and it has been shown that, among instructions given out by trainers of young gladiators was one telling them what to do with a fighter who was *laevus* (the Roman word *sinister*, as has been pointed out, merely meant the left side, not the hand).

The Italian mode of fencing often involved two weapons, sword and short dagger. For the majority, a dagger was naturally held in the left hand (many examples of these daggers can be seen in the Tower of London, and Italian museums). Fencers were thus ambi-dextral. But equally, there were right-handed daggers for sinistral fencers. The element of surprise, and the effect of coming up against the unusual has, of course, always given the left-handed fencer the "edge" on his opponent at their first meeting.

Many world champions in fencing were, and are, left-handed. The sabre Gold Medallist in the 1968 Olympics was left-handed Duma of Rumania. Paul of Britain won the silver medal sinistrally at the 1964 Olympics, and there have been numerous other awards to left-handers.

Left-handed equipment, such as shoulder pads, were originally specially made for the individual, but are now obtainable through the manufacturers.

Hamlet asked, before the fatal bout, "Have all these foils a length?" He might well have asked "Are all these foils right-handed?"

Football
Kicking a ball about has been known since time immemorial, but a game such as Association Football is of comparatively recent origin, and Britain's Cup Final was not inaugurated until 1872. By then, Tom Brown had seen, at Rugby, one of the players pick up the ball and run with it, many years before. American football—the spectacle of which terrifies the British by its apparently meaningless ferocity—began in the 1870s.

For the sinistral, this is obviously a matter of left-footedness. Most good footballers in every branch of the game are to some degree "ambi-footed," as one might describe it, but since left foot and hand are developed, in the sinistral, to a more expert degree than the right, it is easy to see why the left-footed are often placed on the left-hand side of the field, since they can "centre" with greater strength and accuracy.

Well-known international footballers among left-footers include Britain's Bobbie Charlton, Brazil's famous player Pelé, and the Hungarian "Galloping Major," Ferencz Puzcas, who played for the Spanish team Real Madrid.

Golf

This is a Royal and Ancient game indeed, deriving from an old
Dutch word, *kolf*, meaning "club," and although Scotland can
claim to have advanced its popularity, Holland probably created it
in the first instance. The game's wide popularity did not really
start in England or the U.S. until the beginning of the twentieth
century, although long before this, kings like James IV of
Scotland, and Charles I and James II of England, were enthusiastic
players.

Left-handers, of course, could not play the game until recently,
when left-handed clubs were manufactured (it is difficult to determine the exact date). At first they were made to order only, and
were therefore more expensive than the ordinary dextral clubs.
But, thanks to agitation from such bodies as The Left-Handed
Golfers' Club (the late Jack Train—"Colonel Chinstrap" of radio
fame—was at one time President, and was succeeded by the comedian
Ben Warris) it is now possible to buy a sinistral set at no greater cost
than a dextral, and one renowned golfer of today, Bob Charles of
New Zealand, is in the forefront of encouraging other left-handed
golfers in the direction of the champion class.

Hockey

There is, as many schoolgirls and others have pointed out to the
author, no such thing as left-handed hockey. The stick, flat one side
and bevelled the other, can only be used by a right-hander. In
ice-hockey, however, the sinistral can take part, and countries
like Canada include several formidable left-handers among their
experts.

Lawn Tennis

The distinction must be made at once between Royal or "real"
Tennis ("Court" Tennis in the United States) which was played by
King Henry VIII at Hampton Court, and still survives, and Lawn
Tennis, devised in 1874 in England by one Major Walter C.
Wingfield, who applied for a patent to provide "a new and improved
portable court for playing the ancient game of tennis." In the same
year, in the U.S., Miss Mary Outerbridge, after watching British
officers playing lawn tennis at the garrison in Bermuda, introduced

the game to America. The first court was attached to Staten Island Cricket Club. In England, the game was at first called by the unlikely name of Sphairistike ("sticky," for short). In 1877 the impoverished Wimbledon All-England Croquet Club cashed in on the new popularity and the rest is a matter of history. Lawn tennis is a game not much marred by politics, rioting, bottle-throwing or national pride (unlike football and, alas, cricket today) and for years it has been a happy hunting-ground for left-handers. There is no need for special equipment, and the rules provide for as much freedom for the left-hander as the right.

There are, it seems, no famous names of sinistrals in the early years, as with Wilfred Rhodes in cricket, with the exception of the late King George VI, who, as Duke of York, played left-handed in the men's doubles at Wimbledon in 1924. We have to pick up the story with Wimbledon champions such as America's Art ("Tappy") Larsen, an eccentric character who chain-smoked in training, but won the title on his first attempt; "Little Mo" Connolly, women's champion in 1952–53–54, who was left-handed in everything *except* playing tennis; Britain's Kay Stammers (Mrs. Menzies) before the war, and Ann Haydon-Jones after it; Jaroslav Drobny, the exiled Czech who once played for Egypt, and gained the coveted championship at last, in 1954—perhaps the most popular win for a generation.

He has told the author that the secret of success for a left-hander is the back-hand stroke. Left-handed players have to take so many shots on the back-hand that they must develop this stroke to the full if they are to survive.

The measure of left-handed success in comparative proportion to right-handed can be seen in the fact that twice within six years, in 1962 and 1968, the Wimbledon men's singles title has been fought over by two left-handers (all four were Australian). Names such as Rod Laver, recently world champion, Neale Fraser, Tony Roche, and Mervyn Rose from Australia, Roger Taylor and Mark Cox from Britain, Ulrich and Nielson from Denmark, and the two Soviet top players, Lejus and Miss Dimitrieva, are all sinistral.

In similar types of ball-games, the Englishman Jonah Barrington has been world champion in squash and badminton, and left-handed table-tennis champions abound.

SWASTIKA

This symbol is one of the most ancient and significant in world history, once more celebrated than the Cross itself.

The Swastika creates, with its hooked arms, an impression of perpetual motion. When it is hooked in a clock-wise, left-to-right motion it is called a Swastika, a Sanskrit word meaning good fortune, or the spring. It was a symbol of the sun and the worshippers of the sun, and of re-creation. As such, it has been found all over the world, in the Americas, China, Egypt, Palestine, Greece, Scandinavia, Ireland, India, Spain, Mexico, Brittany and many other places.

The opposite of the left-to-right swastika is the suavastika, in which the "wheel" rotates anti-clockwise, and is a symbol, not necessarily of evil, but of the autumnal or setting sun. This "left-handed" swastika is found in Ireland and Scotland, but mainly in Southern India, where there was once a left-handed caste. Rudyard Kipling adopted the suavastika as the symbol printed on the covers of his books. It also appears in China. The British Museum contains the oldest block-printed manuscript in the world, together with the

*Sinistral Swastika
from Troy*

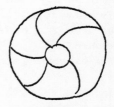

Dextral Swastika (Mayan)

*Lahore, Pakistan:
left-handed Swastika*

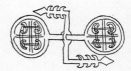

*Left-handed Swastika,
Girvan, Forfarshire (Celtic)*

oldest block-illustration. It is the Diamond Sutra, a Buddhist work transcribed from the sanskrit in A.D. 868 (the Museum even gives the date—11th May). In the illustration an impassive Buddha sits, with a *left*-handed suavastika on his breast, while demons rage around him. This may be due to the fact that this early blockmaker did not realize that blocks *reverse* the image. To the viewer, it is left-handed.

Why did Hitler choose the right-handed swastika as his Nazi party emblem? The story goes back further than Hitler. Buddhism became popular among certain European intellectual groups at the beginning of this century, just as England had a Japanese vogue some years earlier (as reflected in Gilbert and Sullivan's *Mikado*) and the swastika was adopted with it. But the Austrian extremists believed it to be of Indian or Aryan origin, symbolic of racial superiority. Moreover, in Finland and Estonia, it was already a national emblem. Rebellious German troops wore it during the 1920 *putsch*. Finally Hitler adopted it as the symbol of his National Socialist group. In *Mein Kampf* he wrote—

"I have laid down, after countless attempts, the final form of the official flag . . . the swastika, symbolizing the right for victory of Aryan man, and the idea of creative work, which in itself has been eternally anti-semitic and eternally will be anti–semitic."

After World War II, Allied occupation authorities ordered the swastika to be removed from view, and it exists only in the extremist underground nationalist movement, a shameful end to a once world-wide nationalist symbol.

"SWITCHING" OF HANDS

To switch or not to switch? This is a question, as will be seen from evidence of parents elsewhere in this book, which affects parents and teachers all over the world.

In the majority of countries, as we know, right-handed writing is the rule in schools. Therefore the parents, knowing this to be so, may well attempt to persuade a naturally left-handed child to accept preference of the right hand in infancy. If this is done in a practical and sympathetic way, little harm will result, though the child will, in most cases, continue to use the left, preferred hand, or foot, in instinctive actions.

"Switching" of a sinistral child

Such an example is the present Prince of Wales, Prince Charles, who has been seen in newspaper photographs kicking with his left foot in his early schooldays and presenting prizes with his left hand. He plays polo right-handedly (indeed, it is impossible not to) and bats right-handedly in cricket.

But the history of the British Royal Family is several times connected with dual-handedness. Queen Victoria is known to have been ambidextral. An ambidextral painter, Sir Edward Landseer, taught both her and Prince Albert the rudiments of drawing. The crucial moment arrived with the education of Prince Albert, Duke of York, who quite unexpectedly had to assume the throne after the abdication of his brother Edward VIII, as King George VI. His official biographer, Sir John Wheeler-Bennett, asserts that the stammer was due to the treatment given him by a "sadistic and incompetent" governess, when the Prince was about seven or eight years old. He was apparently left-handed naturally but was compelled to change over to the right hand, apparently with little consideration to his feelings in the matter.

This was the era when children's left-handedness was regarded as something peculiar and different. It was no longer regarded as evil, and in league with the devil and witchcraft, as in previous centuries, nor was it connected, as in the Muslim world, with the practice of the Unclean Hand. It was simply non-conformity—and had to be put *right*.

The results on Prince Albert, already, it seems, a highly nervous child, were disastrous. The sadistic governess, whose name has never been disclosed, also ruined his digestion by forcing him to eat his lunch while being driven in a "victoria" carriage. It seems that King George V, whose behaviour towards his children was that of a naval captain on the quarter deck, and Queen Mary, who was German and presumably a supporter of conformity, did nothing to prevent any of this happening, and they did not even sack the governess.

Wheeler-Bennett concludes: "This would create a condition known in psychology as a 'misplaced sinister' and may well have affected the speech."

Those who heard King George VI on public occasions or on radio and TV must have realized what a trial it was for the monarch, who had to speak so many messages of welcome to so many distinguished visitors to his country.

It was only in 1947, when the Royal Family went on their tour of South Africa for several weeks that the British Broadcasting Corporation became concerned about the use of the royal voice. Hitherto any broadcast by the monarch had to be played in full, preceded or followed by the National Anthem. But when the Royal Family left for South Africa in H.M.S. *Vanguard*, the BBC had forgotten to change the rules. A frantic interchange of telephone calls took place between London and Capetown, and eventually it was agreed that the royal voice could be edited—discreetly, not only because of the quality of reception by land-line from South Africa, but because of the monarch's speech disability.

TABLE-MANNERS

For the left-hander, this is not merely a matter of politeness or genteel eating, as with Chaucer's Prioress who ate so daintily she would not let a morsel fall from her lips. It is rather with the layout of the table, the cutlery, and the glasses. All these are done, understandably, for right-handed eating. A large proportion of left-handers have learned to use the knife and fork in the dextral fashion, through the fear at school or the family table of being seen to be "different." But, given a *single* implement, such as a knife for cutting cheese, or a spoon for soup, he will almost invariably revert to the preferred hand, with no great trouble to anyone.

He would also prefer, naturally, to have his glass on the left side. This is permissible at an informal meal, but impossible at a banquet, with the tables set in rows. Wine is traditionally served from the right to the right. To have one's wine-glass on the left is to court

Loyal Toast. Or, more power to which elbow?

disaster with one's neighbour. At a formal dinner, imagine the effect when the loyal toast is called. It might result in dextral and sinistral neighbours reaching out for each other's glasses. The superstitions about drinking toasts come under LUCK (q.v.) but this is purely a matter of geography.

TAPE-RECORDERS

One would not perhaps have thought that these very popular and easily operated machines would be subject to handedness.

Tape spools usually turn clockwise, the magnetic side passing the recording head from left to right. But in a Swiss make, until recently popular as a battery-operated machine, the spools ran anti-clockwise, and a few years ago, the radio reporter Tim Matthews described how a new recorder arrived from the U.S. for inspection by British Broadcasting Corporation experts. Eagerly they crowded round, but were puzzled by the operation of the machine. Eventually someone detected that the manual controls were mainly meant to be operated with the left hand. Upon inquiry, it was found that the recorder had been designed by a left-hander! Only after considerable re-building was it made available for a right-handed world.

The elaborate machines used for transcribing whole books as well as stories and music for people in hospital (The British Library for Hospital Patients, a registered charity) have both a left side and a right side, the left side feeding the type at a standard speed to the right side, which re-records at a non-standard speed, so as to avoid copyright difficulties since it ensures that the tapes, read by professionals, can only be used by the library.

It is odd that handedness can, in fact, invade such a province, which one would have thought would have been entirely dextral. In fact, the operator of a complex machine needs considerable skill and sensitivity in both hands.

TELEPHONE

This invention, by Edison Bell of the United States in 1876, has become one of the machines least favourable to the left-hander.

Consider the situation. In a public telephone box in most countries the machine is situated on the left, as it is on most office desks. Very well: we assume that left-handers have to become left-eared, in

Telephone Game

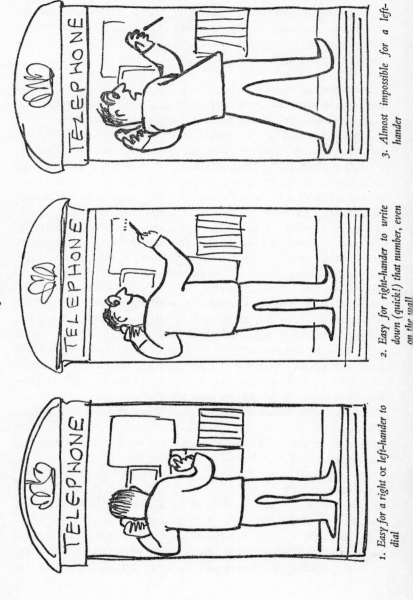

1. Easy for a right or left-hander to dial

2. Easy for right-hander to write down (quick!) that number, even on the wall

3. Almost impossible for a left-hander

picking up the receiver. This leaves them free to dial, or insert money, with the right hand—not a difficult task—but upon receiving a peremptory command, such as "Write down this number quickly —542 1243!" they are unable to do it, without a manual switch-over, which might look funny in a film, but is no fun in real life, as any left-hander knows.

Telephones are usually, in offices, situated similarly on the left-hand side of the desk, with the right hand free for making notes. The left-handed secretary usually replaces the receiver the wrong way round and this may cause trouble with her boss, when the flex gets twisted.

The General Post Office advertises lavishly in order to recruit operators, in Britain. Is one of the questions, "Are you left-handed?" The answer is, yes, and the chances of a real left-hander (not one who has been trained to be ambidextral) getting a job are very small, since the switching operations are done entirely with the right hand. Most telephonists tend to be ambidextral anyhow, so no real problem exists, but the sinistral telephonist would present a real problem if she attempted to do everything left-handedly.

TYPEWRITER

A British patent for such a machine was taken out as early as 1714 by one Henry Mills, but no details remain. Not until the late nineteenth century did C. L. Scholes of Milwaukee produce an instrument faster than the pen and capable of mass production. It was manufactured by the Remington Armoury. Though it printed capitals only, and the results could not immediately be read, the keyboard, designed to keep the most-used letters apart, remains almost unaltered to this day.

Handedness comes in for the typewriter in two ways. The more important controls on a non-electric machine are inclined to be on the *left* side, and it has been proved, after exhaustive tests by researchers of Sir Isaac Pitman & Sons Ltd., that, on the English keyboard, the ratio of left- to right-hand usage is 14:12. Therefore the left hand is working harder. Experiments are now continuing, using other languages.

This interesting fact may account for the excellence of the work of many left-handed typists, including champions!

UNIVERSE, THE

Is the universe left-handed? In his fascinating book *The Ambidextrous Universe*, Martin Gardner, popular American writer on mathematics and science, began investigating the importance of the discovery, by the Chinese-born American physicists, Lee and Young (both Nobel prize winners) that parity—that is, symmetry or equality—between left and right in the universe as a whole were not guaranteed. Non-symmetry was more likely. Gardner reported: "The news flashed from laboratory to laboratory that parity is not conserved. Professors waved their arms, and talked excitedly about spin, about mirrors, and anti-worlds, and even undergraduates sensed that something was afoot."

There are, Gardner says, four fundamental types of forces governing the universe as we know it. Nuclear force, electromagnetic force, weak interaction force and gravitational force. Three had hitherto seemed to work according to symmetrical pattern, but the third, the weak interaction force—weaker than electro-magnetism but stronger than gravity—though known to exist, had remained a mystery. Now it was described as having a left-right difference, with a preference for the left, in an historical paper called "Question of Parity Conservation in Weak Interactions."

The exciting story was taken up by another Chinese-born American, Madame Chien-Shiung Wu, of Columbia University, the world's leading woman physicist. Her experiment is too technical to describe here, but it involved a nucleus of cobalt (which is a white magnetic metal resembling iron) which normally shot out electrons equally in a northerly and southerly direction. Madame Wu had the cobalt nucleus cooled down to zero, and then the surprise came: the main issue of electrons came from the south, or left side!

This was unexpected news for the theoretical physicists. One of the most famous, Professor Pauli of Zürich, had previously been sceptical about the experiment, and had said, "I do *not* believe that the Lord is a weak left-hander, and I am ready to bet a very high sum that the experiments will give symmetrical results."

When they didn't, and the south or left side appeared dominant, he admitted "I am shocked not so much by the fact that the Lord prefers the left hand as by the fact that he still appears to be left-handed symmetric."

So, if this be a predominantly right-handed world, that world is still a tiny planet in a multitudinous universe, one of whose forces is left-handed. Take heart, again, sinistrals, as we begin to leave earth and explore the universe. Take heed, Lord: your alleged authority in this matter is being threatened.

Mr. Gardner adds a practical note—

"The right-handedness of screw and bolt threads reflects the dominant right-handedness of the human race. If you hold a screwdriver in your right hand, a stronger twisting force can be exerted clockwise than anti-clockwise because it brings the powerful biceps muscles into play. In addition, the fleshy base of the right thumb applies greater frictional resistance to the screwdriver handle when it is twisted clockwise."

WEAPONS
These are mainly intended for right-handed use. It was Thomas Carlyle's view that dextrality "might have arisen in primitive fighting, with the shield held in the left hand, to protect the heart and its adjacencies."

This theory had been denied more than two hundred years earlier by Sir Thomas Browne, who claimed that the heart was not entirely on the left side, but only very slightly so, and that the superstitions about protecting your "left-sided heart" was merely another Vulgar Error. The tradition, however, has persisted, and man has gone out to fight with his right "sword-arm," principally because he is predominantly a right-handed person. One of the main rules of battle, as laid down by King Richard I (Richard Cœur de Lion) was that troops should go into action from right to left, protecting with the sinister shield, attacking with the dextral sword, lance, etc. It was Napoleon who reversed this battle order in days when cannon had partially replaced manual weapons and could fire in any direction, thereby winning some of his most famous victories.

From the earliest days, the left-handed fighter enjoyed his own particular reputation. The Lord God of Israel chose Ehud the Benjamite, "a man left-handed," to take the King of Moab by surprise and stab him. In ancient Rome, trainers of gladiators gave out special instructions to their already luckless trainees on what to do when faced with a "southpaw" gladiator, of whom there were apparently many, whose actions with sword, net, trident and mace were very skilful.

Left-handed swordsmen and fencers were also highly valued, as we have seen. The two-handed sword-and-dagger play was particularly popular. Normally the dagger would be the left-handed weapon: there are many such wicked-looking specimens in the Tower of London and in Naples Museum. The surprise came when the swordsman produced his rapier in the left hand and his specially-shaped dagger in his right.

It is a premiss of military discipline and practice that the right hand and eye shall be dominant, though the practice of "dressing by the right" and the "left-right" system of marching were comparatively late in their introduction. As long ago as 4000 B.C., Noah complained that, of the population of Nineveh, no man knew his left hand from his right. It is thought that the Roman legionaries may have marched "left-right" but there is the well-known dilemma of the Scottish troops (and many English, too) who had to have hay tied to one foot and straw to the other, and march "hay-foot, straw-foot."

The left-foot-first is not only the instinctive step of the majority of bipeds (including penguins) as opposed to the right-left of quadrupeds. It is the logical movement of the warrior who bore arms on the right side and a shield on the left. Scabbards, of course, were on the left, but the sword was drawn with the dextral "sword-arm."

The story of rifles and their ejector systems has long made the life of left-handed, and left-eyed recruits a misery.

"WIDDERSHINS"

This is one of the important terms every left-hander must know. It is the opposite of the Circumambulation of sun-worshippers and most religions, because it is, as far as the northern hemisphere of the world is concerned, anti-sunwards and anti-clockwise.

Although it survives mainly in Scotland, the word "widdershins" is of German origin, and means *widersin*, "against the direction." Scottish folklore abounds in superstitions about movements (see CIRCUMAMBULATION). Funeral processions had to make their way from left to right, unless, in certain occasions, it was deliberately

Go well—go Widdershins!

made widdershins, in order to appease or confound the evil spirits. "To move against the sun," wrote Ira S. Wile, "was to exhibit respect for Satan, in much the same way as repeating the Lord's prayer backwards was supposed to do."

This backwards-motion is all part of the Black Magic cult which still occurs occasionally today, and is obviously connected directly with Devil-worship, but only indirectly with left-handedness. The Oxford English Dictionary has a number of early references to the cult of "widdershins," as follows—

1545: "The said Margaret Balfour was ane huyr [whore] and ane wyche, and went widdershins about nine hours sark alone."

1583: "The venerable virgins whom we wold call witches, nine times widdershins about the thorn raid."

1596: "The blade of the corn grows withersons, and when it growis . . . it will be any guid chaip [cheap] year."

1624: At the Orkney Witch Trial: "He gang thrys witherwards about the cow, and straik hir the left syde."

1685: "The men turned nine times widdershins about, and the women six times" (G. Sinclair, *Satan's Invisible World*.)

Finally, Rudyard Kipling (*The Five Nations*): "So widdershins circling the bride bed of death."

ZANGWILL, PROFESSOR

Oliver Zangwill, Professor in the Department of Experimental Psychology at Cambridge, has been in the forefront in challenging the traditional acceptance of cerebral dominance or crossed laterality. After a prolonged examination of head-injury cases, conducted in Oxford with Dr. Humphrey, he declared in a paper: "No longer can the human race be viewed as divided into two mutually exclusive categories—sinister and right-brained, dexter and left-brained. Handedness must be regarded as a graded characteristic. Indeed, cerebral dominance itself is in all probability a graded characteristic, varying in scope and completeness from individual to individual. Its precise relation to handedness still needs to be ascertained."

So let the last word in this Dictionary, from A to Z, be with Professor Zangwill. So long as there are experts willing to pursue the question of right- and left-handedness, in all its implications, throughout all walks of life, man may do right by the left after all.

The Left-hander and the Future

Sinistrality is an anatomic compulsion under the direction of inherent nervous controls, that should not be disregarded. The rights of minorities should be respected, and the right of the left hand to normal expression should be encouraged and not denied

IRA S. WILE

In this survey of Left-handed Man in a Right-handed World, we have tried to keep in every way a sense of proportion. The numerical proportion can either be based on the flat 8 per cent of the *Encyclopædia Britannica*, or it can be enlarged to the 30 per cent of Dr. Bryngelson of Minnesota. Somewhere between these two figures the answer lies, but it is not merely numerical proportions which have inspired this further inquiry into sinistrality. Many right-handers have told the author that they never thought about the subject until it was mentioned: thereafter, they have seen left-handers everywhere, and have taken note of their occasional plight in grappling with a dextral world. This is all to the good, and reminds right-handers that this complex civilization in which we live can be made easier for the minority of sinistrals by just a few inventions and adaptations in daily life.

This is where the pioneers come into being, such as the recent venture called *Anything Left-Handed*.

In October, 1968, the first shop in the world catering exclusively for left-handers opened in London, and some visitors were surprised to find how many different articles, ranging from a potato-peeler to a full-scale carpenter's bench, were available. (It came as no surprise to sinistrals who had so often sought out items like scissors with the cutting edge on the appropriate side.)

The founder, Mr. William Gruby, himself right-handed, conceived the idea following a dinner party at which he found that all his four guests were left-handed, and all willing to complain bitterly about the lack of provision made for sinistrals in a dextral world. His own private researches among shop-assistants revealed little but sarcasm. When he once asked for the left-handed tin-opener, the reply was, "Would you like a left-handed tin to go with it?" But it was different when Mr. Gruby got to grips with the manufacturers.

"Their initial reaction was, what a good idea to make things for the left-handed minority.

"A fountain-pen manufacturer was very glad we were getting a sales outlet for his left-handed pen, because he'd sold 20,000 of them already.

"But on the whole, manufacturers were a little bit reluctant about creating anything new, and you can understand their point of view.

"The most interested people, of course," he went on, "were those you couldn't at first get hold of—the actual designers. You were sent off to the sales people, and they, of course, only interested in something which can already be proved to have a market. It's an entirely different approach."

Mr. Gruby had recently received an ambidextral pepper-mill, made in France, which worked equally well when twisted with either hand. He had shown this to a British manufacturer, who took it to pieces to examine the mechanism, and then conferred with some of his colleagues. We may, therefore, see a pepper-mill for operation by left-handers in Britain, and later in other countries. A small instance, but a logical one. If a piece of equipment can be worked with the right hand, why not with the left as well?

The venture is not, as Mr. Gruby says, "a unique left-handed aspect." He would not sell a make of entirely left-handed potato-peelers (this is one of the stock grievances of the sinistral and may well date back, not only to the housewife but to the left-handed lower ranks of the Armed Forces condemned to a period of "spud-bashing.")

An ambidextral make supplies the answer and this, in his opinion, applies to a number of household objects, such as a saucepan which has a lip on both sides and can be poured equally well with either hand.

There are certain objects, such as a T-square for designers, an artist's palette with a hole for the thumb, and a pair of scissors which, functionally, must be operated by one of the two hands, and these are now available for unilateral, left-handed use only.

"I have," says Mr. Gruby, "been able to get salesmen to go back into the bowels of their business, and discuss this left-handed question, perhaps for the first time ever."

A general recognition of left-handedness as a natural and not unimportant function was necessary, he agreed, before the special needs of the left-hander could be satisfied—so that "a man in Newcastle, shall we say, could walk into an ironmonger's shop and just ask for a left-handed implement, just like that." Unless there is this recognition, the main manufacturers would, of course, not be interested, because the returns would not be worth while.

The other production problem is the continuation of a certain specialized line for a minority demand—a "flow-line" as Mr. Gruby called it. Economically, it would be possible for a thousand or so articles to be manufactured on a single occasion not to be repeated, but there are obvious problems in keeping up a regular supply. The one advantage for a manufacturer who went in for supplying a range of articles for left-handed or ambidextral use is that there would be practically no competition. The field would be his.

It will be interesting to see whether, in the years to come, the unique venture by the Left-Handed Shop in London will lead to permanent and widening help for sinistrals unable to adapt themselves to dextral appliances.

Is chronicling the history, the achievements and the problems of the left-handed minority worth while? There are many indications that it is. As has been said, this is a minority which will, presumably, continue so long as the human race exists. The universe itself, as Martin Gardner has pointed out, has no exact parity—it may well be biased towards the left. Hurrah, cries the left-hander, with one faint cheer. It's just as well that there are writers, education experts, psychiatrists—and artists—who are interested in the sinistral side of life. Left, as it were, on his own, the right-hander seems to remain ignorant of the whole subject until he is reminded of it, and then one discovers, in so many cases, that there is a sinistral member of the family, or a relation who (now they come to think of it) is left-handed.

No one would pretend, as has been pointed out, that the left-hander, in any civilized, up-to-date country, is subject to the persecutions of the past. But it is also true that, in the majority of countries in the world, left-handed writing is not permitted in schools, and this is one of the primary points of the left-handed attitude: it should be permitted. Experts like Dr. Macdonald Critchley believe it should be allowed, and there would seem to be no case for forbidding it, in any country. If sportsmen are allowed freedom to play games and win championships and Olympic Gold Medals with the left hand, why should not left-handed handwriting be allowed also? This is one of the major aims of the left-handed minority—freedom to write, as well as freedom to play cricket, baseball, lawn tennis and other games. To "switch" a left-hander, as we have seen, can be accompanied by speech and nervous troubles. The answer is, don't do it. Leave the natural left-hander to do as he likes, provided his sinistrality is not accompanied by any neurological or other difficulties. Left-handedness, as Dr. Wile has pointed out, is instinctive. Interfere with it, and you do so at your peril, as far as the child is concerned. It is a natural trait, and with so many left-handed experts in the world, in proportion to their minority number, the right-hander had better look to his laurels!

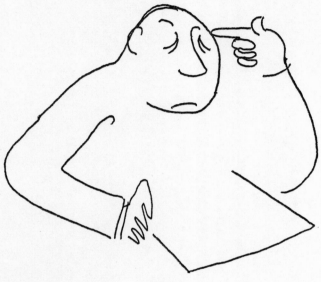

The End

Appendix: Left-handed Organizations

The International Society of Left-Handers (U.S.A.)
President: Adolph G. Miller
Treasurer: Steven G. Miller
Loves Park, Illinois, U.S.

The Left-Handers' Association (U.K.)
Founder and Secretary: Michael Barsley, Oxford, England.

The Irish Left-Handed Association
Founder: Noel Jones, 16 Mount Pleasant Square, Dublin, Eire.

"Anything Left-Handed" Ltd., specialists in left-handed implements.
Directors: William & Claudia Gruby, Beak Street, London W.1,
England.

Bibliography

The following books are among those which I have consulted in compiling the present work. Some belong to history, and would be of little practical use to those studying the problems and possibilities of left-handedness.

For them I suggest, as works which are useful, helpful, and probably obtainable in libraries, such studies as Sir Cyril Burt's *The Backward Child*; Dr. Margaret Clark's *Left-Handedness*; Martin Gardner's recent and exhilarating *The Ambidextrous Universe* (which is not primarily about left-handedness, but knocks a hole in dextral complacency); and C. S. Orton's *Reading, Writing and Speech Problems in Children*.

BLAU, ABRAM. *The Master Hand.* American Orthopsychiatric Association, New York, 1946.

BRAIN, LORD. *Speech Disorders.* Butterworth, London, 1961.

BROWNE, SIR THOMAS. *Pseudoxia Epidemia,* or "Enquiries into Very Many Received Tenets and Commonly Presum'd TRUTHS which examined prove but VULGAR ERRORS." London, 1648.

BURT, SIR CYRIL. *The Backward Child.* University of London Press, 1957.

CAMPBELL, J. G. *Superstitions of Scotland.* Glasgow, 1900.

CHAPLIN, CHARLES. *My Autobiography.* Simon & Schuster, New York, 1964.

CHRISTIAENS, L. and others. *Les Gauchers au Travail.* Journées Nationales de Médecine de Travail, Masson, Paris, 1962.

CLARK, MARGARET. *Left-Handedness.* University of London Press, 1957.

COLE, L. *Psychology of the Elementary School Subjects.* Farrar & Rinehart, New York, 1934.

CRITCHLEY, MACDONALD. *Mirror Writing.* Kegan Paul, London, 1928. *The Black Hole and Other Essays,* Pitman Medical, London, 1964.

CROWLEY, ALEISTER. *Magic in Theory and Practice.* Privately printed at the Lecram Press, Paris, 1929.

CUNNINGHAM, J. T. *Natural History of Marine Fishes.* Macmillan, London, 1896.

DEE, DR. JOHN. *Private Diary* (edition of 1842).

ELWORTHY, F. T. *The Evil Eye.* John Murray, London, 1895.
Encyclopaedia Britannica.

GARDNER, MARTIN. *The Ambidextrous Universe.* Penguin Press, London, 1964.
GESELL, ARNOLD. *The First Five Years of Life.* Methuen, London, 1954.
GLANVILL, JOSEPH. *Saducismus Triumphatus.* London, 1689.
GUAZZO, MARIE FRANCESCO. *Compendium Maleficarum.* Rodker, London, 1929.

HANNAH, WALTON. *Darkness Visible.* Augustine Press, London, 1954.
HERODOTUS. *Histories.* John Murray, London, 1862.
HERTZ, ROBERT. *Death and the Right Hand.* Cohen & West, London, 1960.
HILL, DOUGLAS, and WILLIAMS, PAT. *The Supernatural.* Aldus Books, London,
    1965.

JACKSON, JOHN. *Ambidexterity.* Kegan Paul, London, 1905.
JONES, BERNARD. *Freemasons' Guide.* Harrap, London, 1950.
JUNG, KARL. *Aion.* Routledge, Kegan Paul, London, 1959. *Practice of Psycho-*
    therapy.

KAY, JAMES DE. *The Left-Handed Book.* Evans, New York, 1966.

LOMBROSO, CESARE. *Left Sidedness.* North American Review, 1903.

MAPLE, ERIC. *The Dark World of Witches.* Robert Hale, London, 1962.
MEREJOWSKI, DMITRI. *The Romance of Leonardo da Vinci.* Modern Library, New
    York, 1928.
MURRAY, DR. MARGARET. *Witch-Cult in Western Europe.* Oxford University
    Press, 1921.

NAIDOO, S. *Laterality.* University of London Thesis, 1961.

ORTON, C. S. *Reading, Writing and Speech Problems in Children.* Chapman &
    Hall, London, 1937.

PARSON, BEAUFORT SIMS. *Left-Handedness.* The Macmillan Co., New York,
    1924.
PARTRIDGE, ERIC. *Dictionary of Slang and Unconventional Usage.* Oxford
    University Press, London.

RIPER, C. VAN. *Speech Correction.* Prentice-Hall, New York, 1947.

SELIGMANN, KURT. *The History of Magic.* Pantheon Books, New York, 1948.
STODDARD, ASHWELL. *Treatise on Moles.* Hudson, New York, 1805.

TRAVIS, EDWARD LEE. *Speech Pathology.* Appleton & Co., New York, 1931.

TSAI, L. S. and MAURER, S. "Right-Handedness in White Rats." *Science*, vol. lxxii, 1930.

WEDECK, HARRY E. *A Treasury of Witchcraft*. Philosophical Library, New York, 1961.

WESTERMARCK, EDWARD. *Ritual and Belief in Morocco*. Macmillan, London, 1926.

WHEELER-BENNETT, SIR JOHN. *King George VI*. Macmillan, London, 1958.

WILE, IRA S. *Handedness, Right and Left*. Lothrop, Lee & Shepard Co., Boston, 1934.

WILSON, COLIN. "My Search for Jack the Ripper." *Evening Standard*, London, 6th August, 1960.

WILSON, SIR DANIEL. *Left-Handedness*. Nature Series, Macmillan, London, 1891.

ZANGWILL, OLIVER. *Cerebral Dominance and its Relation to Psychological Function*. Oliver and Boyd, Edinburgh, 1960.

Index

THE LEFT-HANDED BOOK

by

MICHAEL BARSLEY

THE LEFT-HANDED BOOK was the first study of the history of left-handedness. It provides the material for serious study of an engrossing subject in a light-hearted way. Michael Barsley exposes the centuries-old conspiracy to deprive left-handed people of their rights as citizens. Even the words "their rights" emphasizes the great gulf between the two. He points out that since the Bible clearly divided us into sheep and goats, and put the goats on the left, right-handers have acted as though all left-handers were to be despised. And left-handers number about 8 per cent of the population.

"Barsley became so steamed up about the persecution of sinistrals that he resolved to write a book. The result after 15 years' hard research is a most fascinating and unusual investigation."—Peter Grosvenor in the DAILY EXPRESS.

"It's going to be very useful to have such a formidable body of evidence as Mr. Barsley has collected to fire back at my future persecutors."—Max Hastings in the EVENING STANDARD.

"The hard-core sinistrals have shown their worth by holding out so long against adroit and dexterous forms of discrimination. Mr Barsley's admirably uprighteous book should inspire them to stand up and fight for their lefts." —THE ECONOMIST.

Published by SOUVENIR PRESS LTD., 95 Mortimer Street, London, W.1

29 illustrations   *4 drawings*   *240 pages*   *30s.*